THE ELIJAH TAPESTRY

John 1 and 21

Mystery, Majesty and Mathematics in John's Gospel #1

ANNE HAMILTON

The Elijah Tapestry—John 1 and 21:
Mystery, Majesty and Mathematics in John's Gospel #1

© Anne Hamilton 2023
Published by Armour Books
P. O. Box 492, Corinda QLD 4075 Australia

Cover image composite: Lucky Girl Creative © 2020, Cottage Arts © 2019, Forever Artisan 6 © 2023 courtesy of Forever.com; Adobe Stock | Nimer
Cover & Interior Design and Typeset by Beckon Creative

ISBN: 978-1-925380-53-8

A catalogue record for this book is available from the National Library of Australia

All rights reserved. No part of this publication may be reproduced, stored in, or introduced into a retrieval system, or transmitted, in any form, or by any means (electronic, mechanical, photocopying, recording or otherwise) without the prior written permission of the publisher.

Note: Australian spelling and grammar conventions are used throughout this book.

The cover image features pools in Wadi Al-Rayyan in Jordan. Wadi Ali-Rayyan was until recently known as Wadi Al-Yabis. In ancient times, it was the Brook Cherith that sheltered Elijah. It was where John the Baptist began his ministry.

Unless otherwise noted, Scripture quotations are taken from The Holy Bible, Berean Study Bible, BSB Copyright ©2016 by Bible Hub Used by Permission. All Rights Reserved Worldwide.

Scripture quotations marked AMP are taken from the Amplified Version of the Bible Copyright © 2015 by The Lockman Foundation, La Habra, CA 90631. All rights reserved. www.lockman.org

Scripture quotations marked ASV are taken from the American Standard Version of the Bible. Public domain.

Scripture quotations marked BLB are taken from the The Blue Letter Bible. Used by permission. blueletterbible.org

Scripture quotations marked BSB are taken from the The Holy Bible, Berean Study Bible, BSB Copyright ©2016 by Bible Hub Used by Permission. All Rights Reserved Worldwide.

Scripture quotations marked CEV are from the Contemporary English Version Copyright © 1991, 1992, 1995 by American Bible Society. Used by Permission.

Scripture quotations marked CSB are taken The Christian Standard Bible. Copyright © 2017 by Holman Bible Publishers. Used by permission. Christian Standard Bible®, and CSB® are federally registered trademarks of Holman Bible Publishers, all rights reserved.

Scripture quotations marked ESV are taken from the ESV® Bible (The Holy Bible, English Standard Version®), copyright © 2001 by Crossway, a publishing ministry of Good News Publishers. Used by permission. All rights reserved.

Scripture quotations marked GNT are from the Good News Translation in Today's English Version—Second Edition Copyright © 1992 by American Bible Society. Used by Permission.

Scripture quotations marked GWT are taken from GOD'S WORD®, a copyrighted work of God's Word to the Nations. Quotations are used by permission. Copyright 1995 by God's Word to the Nations. All rights reserved.

Scripture quotations marked HCSB are taken from the Holman Christian Standard Bible®, Used by Permission HCSB ©1999,2000,2002,2003,2009 Holman Bible Publishers. Holman Christian Standard Bible®, Holman CSB®, and HCSB® are federally registered trademarks of Holman Bible Publishers.

Scripture quotations marked ISV are taken from the Holy Bible: International Standard Version®. Copyright © 1996-forever by The ISV Foundation. ALL RIGHTS RESERVED INTERNATIONALLY. Used by permission.

Scripture quotations marked KJV are taken from the King James Version of the Bible. Public domain.

Scripture quotations marked NASB are taken from the New American Standard Bible®, Copyright © 1960, 1962, 1963, 1968, 1971, 1972, 1973, 1975, 1977, 1995 by The Lockman Foundation. Used by permission. (www.Lockman.org)

Scripture quotations marked NLT are taken from the Holy Bible, New Living Translation, copyright 1996, 2004. Used by permission of Tyndale House Publishers, Inc., Wheaton, Illinois 60189. All rights reserved.

Scripture quotations marked NIV are taken from the Holy Bible, New International Version®, NIV®. Copyright © 1973, 1978, 1984, 2011 by Biblica, Inc.™ Used by permission of Zondervan. All rights reserved worldwide. www.zondervan.com The "NIV" and "New International Version" are trademarks registered in the United States Patent and Trademark Office by Biblica, Inc.™.

Scripture quotations marked NKJV are taken from the New King James Version. Copyright © 1982 by Thomas Nelson, Inc. Used by permission. All rights reserved.

Scripture quotations marked NRS are taken from New Revised Standard Version of the Bible, copyright 1952 [2nd edition, 1971] by the Division of Christian Education of the National Council of the Churches of Christ in the United States of America. Used by permission. All rights reserved.

Scripture quotations marked PHPS are taken from the New Testament in Modern English © 1958, 1959, 1960 J.B. Phillips and 1947, 1952, 1955, 1957 The Macmillan Company, New York. Used by permission. All rights reserved.

Scripture quotations marked WEB are taken from the World English Bible, a modernisation of the American Standard Version (ASV). Public domain.

Scripture quotations marked WEY are taken from the Weymouth New Testament. Public domain.

Table of Contents

	Preamble	9
	Preface	11
	Introduction	13
Part 1		18
1.1	The Scribe	21
1.2	Numerical Literary Style	25
1.3	Poetry of the Prophets	31
1.4	The Mirror Summarised	37
Part 2		44
2.1	Poet and Poem	47
2.2	The Cosmic Canticle	50
2.3	'Unnecessary' Words	53
2.4	The Golden Ratio	58
2.5	The Golden Beginning	62
2.6	Creation's Clothing	64
2.7	The Healing Tree	70
Part 3		74
3.1	An Abominable Beauty	77
3.2	A Splash of Seventeens	80
Part 4		88
4.1	The Light of the World	91
4.2	The Coming of Immanuel	94
4.3	Proclaiming Perfection	97
4.4	Children of God	100
4.5	Hidden Elegance	103
4.6	Children of Light	107
4.7	Big Fish and Little Fish	109
4.8	Two Witnesses	113
4.9	Moses and Elijah	116

Part 5 — 120

- 5.1 We Have Seen His Glory — 123
- 5.2 The Only — 126
- 5.3 Death and Honour — 128
- 5.4 Mathematics Became Man — 130
- 5.5 The Fire in the Equations — 132

Part 6 — 138

- 6.1 Enfolded by Grace — 141
- 6.2 Elijah's Mantle — 144
- 6.3 Out in the Wilderness — 146
- 6.4 On Top of the Temple — 150

Part 7 — 154

- 7.1 The Four Craftsmen — 157
- 7.2 Three Questions by the Water — 160
- 7.3 Elijah's Unfinished Task — 167
- 7.4 Love, Love, Love — 175
- 7.5 Identity and Identification — 179
- 7.6 The Voice — 182

Part 8 — 184

- 8.1 Side, Sandals and Fish — 187
- 8.2 The Sandal: Conquest and Romance — 192
- 8.3 Immanuel, the Fish and the Logos — 195
- 8.4 Archimedes and the 'Measure of the Fish' — 197
- 8.5 The Inheritors — 200
- 8.6 The Waters of Wadi Al-Yabis — 204
- 8.7 *Is* and *Is Not* — 207
- 8.8 The Crushed Head and the Bruised Heel — 212
- 8.9 The Name of God — 217

Part 9 — 222

- 9.1 Recognition and Identification — 225
- 9.2 Lambs of God — 228
- 9.3 Doubly Forgiven — 230
- 9.4 The Sail and the Net — 232
- 9.5 The Long-Awaited Anointing — 236

Part 10 — 242

- 10.1 Recognition — 245
- 10.2 Bethsaida — 248
- 10.3 The 'Five' — 250

Part 11		254
11.1	The Writings	257
11.2	Son of Joseph	260
Part 12		264
12.1	Doubts	269
12.2	Introductions, Inheritance and Identity	272
12.3	Ascending	276
12.4	The Emmaus Mending	280
12.5	Full Circle	286

Preamble

Around the world many people participate annually in *NaNoWriMo*—National Novel Writing Month. They set aside time each day in November towards reaching a certain target, a particular word-count by the end of the month. In 2021, I decided to set myself a non-fiction goal for November and write a small booklet on the parallel elements that I'd noticed in the first and last chapters of John's gospel. It shouldn't take me too long—that's what I thought. There's a few broad brushstroke themes I can highlight and it'll be a wrap. I might even be able to knock this off in a few days if I get my act together.

That's how I approached the task. Now it took about ten minutes to disabuse myself of the naïvety of this thinking. As soon as I got serious about looking at the very first and very last verses of the gospel, I realised the mirror structure was far more extensive than I'd previously thought. My small booklet quickly morphed into this full-size volume about ten times the size I'd anticipated.

And it also hit a roadbump. As the questions of identity came thick and fast in the gospel, at the same time questions of identity arose about the book itself. What was it? My purpose in writing is not academic, it's devotional. I want my books to open up and deepen your relationship with Jesus—to inform your mind, so that your heart and soul leap and turn to Him in recognition of new revelation that, paradoxically, you've always known. So I don't want to present you with watered-down skim-milk that satisfies neither mind nor heart. Nor do I want to serve up meat so tough and chewy that it's impossible to digest intellectually.

Consequently, this book is an uneasy balance between scholarly and prayerful. I know I haven't got it right. So I ask your indulgence regarding its awkward nature and its attempt to sit on the fence between academic and devotional.

Preface

This book is designed for anyone wanting to explore the deeps of the fourth gospel in a different way. It's for readers who want to dip their toes into academic scholarship while still reclining in a pool of theology that is primarily devotional in nature.

That's very much my own preference. I like tough, challenging writing that compels me to examine my own life in the light of the Scriptural record. And the older I get, the more important I realise it is to do hard stuff. If we don't extend ourselves intellectually, we gradually lose our ability to push ourselves and even our memories are affected. If we don't extend ourselves spiritually, the same is true. To grow, we have to constantly seek new frontiers within ourselves as well as externally, not settling for the comfort of the familiar. The quest to understand the messages God has put in His Word is not one we can leave to others.

The Elijah Tapestry forms a record of my quest through the first 51 verses of John's gospel as well as the corresponding 39 verses at the end. So, although the title of this book suggests I am restricting myself to the final chapter, actually I've ventured backwards 13 verses into chapter 20.

Now I don't doubt I've missed a lot of interconnections between these sections. If you spot any, I'd love to know what you find.

Please don't hesitate to contact me with your insights. As I've been inspired by the writings of others, I trust that in turn you will be inspired to unlock doors in Scripture that have been rusted shut for centuries.

At first, when I began looking for the matches between the beginning and end of John's gospel, I was just interested in the broad concentric brushstrokes. However, as I examined individual verses more closely, it quickly became obvious even the finer details were arranged very precisely. The symmetry of themes is not flawless in texture but it's certainly exquisite.

Once the subtle references to Elijah in the last chapter became clear, the parallelism was almost perfect—except for one gap in the line-up. Now, if there'd been more than one, I might have let the matter slide, but just one by itself suggested I was missing something critical. Eventually it dawned on me that the text itself was posing a riddle: 'Why is a loose sandal like a net full of 153 fish?'

I don't doubt that was a rip-roaringly funny joke twenty centuries ago but it's completely lost its humour in the intervening time. However, if you'd like to know the answer to this ancient brainteaser, read on.

Anne Hamilton
Seventeen Mile Rocks, Australia
New Year's Eve, 2021

Introduction

The gospel of John is a masterwork of literature. It was written towards the end of the first century, with the intention of introducing Jesus, a man who had lived and worked in Galilee some decades previously, to a Greek audience. John had known Jesus first-hand for about three years and wanted to bear witness to events he'd personally observed.

He might have chosen to write a straight-forward biography, similar to the synoptic gospels, in order to testify to his faith. Instead his memoir is an impeccably crafted poem. It revealed that, through a divine irruption across the margin between heaven and earth, the creator of the world was born into it to save it. The message of life and hope John proclaimed concerned the coming of the Messiah.

However, the beloved apostle faced an almost insurmountable dilemma. This particular problem had been barely a blip on the horizon for a previous herald—his namesake John the Baptiser. The concept of the 'Messiah' that was anchored soul-deep in the Jews was utterly meaningless to the Greeks. The profound, passionate longing for national salvation and spiritual healing that a mere mention of the Messiah evoked in Hebrew listeners contrasted with shrugging indifference on the part of the Gentiles.

Paul had already made clear the cultural chasm separating Jews and Greeks:

> *'Jews ask for signs, and Greeks look for wisdom.'*
>
> 1 Corinthians 1:22[ISV]

Finding common ground between these vastly different cultures was supremely difficult. Yet, as William Barclay has pointed out, John came up with a consummately inspired solution. He used a term with significant overtones for both Jews and Greeks—thus speaking deeply to both audiences. His solution to the problem was exceptional: to bring to the fore a concept with a rich and meaningful background in both cultures—*the Word*.

John seized on the Greek term LOGOS which, so Barclay said, means two things—*word* and *reason*. The splendid and dependable arrangement of the cosmos resulted from the majestic order of the mind of God—itself the source of *reason*. John was effectively saying to the Greeks, 'All your lives you have been fascinated by this great, guiding, controlling mind of God. The mind of God has come to earth in the man Jesus. Look at Him and you will see what the mind and thought of God are like.'[1]

Barclay also pointed out the equivalent Hebrew word, *dabar*, indicated far more than a mere sound. He quoted John Paterson: 'The spoken word to the Hebrew was fearfully alive… It was a unit of energy charged with power. It flies like a bullet to its billet.'[2]

John's solution was genius, pure and simple. However, the choice of LOGOS was not without significant problems. It was a complex term that, despite Barclay's confident assertion it had two

---

[1] William Barclay, *The Gospel of John Volume 1*, The Daily Study Bible, The Saint Andrew Press Edinburgh 1963, p xxiii

[2] William Barclay, *The Gospel of John Volume 1*, The Daily Study Bible, The Saint Andrew Press Edinburgh 1963, p 3

meanings—*word* and *reason*—actually was not limited to just those options.³ Most notable amongst the other meanings was *ratio*.

As you may suspect, this is a technical term straight from mathematics. Importantly, it was in the sphere of geometry and arithmetic that the full ramifications of the Greek understanding of the 'mind of God' came into play. The Greeks interpretated mathematics in a religious framework and, for them, the *Logos* had overtones of godhood. For believers educated in Platonic philosophy, the *Logos* would have evoked ideal forms and deified numbers.

'No one expects the days to be gods,' said Ralph Waldo Emerson.

Neither does anyone, in our present era, normally ever suspect that, in the past, certain numbers were viewed as gods in their own right. Yet, even in this century, there's been a spectacular instance when the *Logos* underwent an explosive resurgence in popularity. Hundreds of millions of people read *The Da Vinci Code* with its exposition of the *Logos*—better known today as the golden ratio—as a pervading spiritual force.

There's a good reason the *Logos* has an inherent appeal to the human heart. Back when John was writing, THE *Logos* wasn't simply a mathematical expression. Just as today it is considered a sacred number in some circles, it was then seen as divine in nature.

It was an integral feature in the worship of Pythagoras—the philosopher who introduced quadratic equations to Europe and who probably made your life difficult in high school algebra with

---

3 Brian Simmons also suggests that it means two things—his choices are *message* and *blueprint*—and he translates LOGOS as 'Living Expression'. He does not note the mathematical overtones of the word but says: Jesus 'is the divine self-expression of all that God is, contains and reveals in incarnated flesh. Just as we express ourselves in words, God has perfectly expressed Himself in Christ.' *The Book of John: Eternal Love*, Second Edition, BroadStreet Publishing Group LLC, 2019

a theorem about right-angled triangles. Pythagoras left behind a Brotherhood who considered their founder to be a god. And when members of this mystic religion of numbers and forms became acquainted with Christianity, they quickly reached what was, for them, an obvious conclusion: Pythagoras of Samos had been reincarnated as Jesus of Nazareth.

This was a critical problem, since the Good News—being utterly dependent on the resurrection of Christ—would be completely undermined by the Pythagorean notion of transmigration of souls. Reincarnation and resurrection are totally incompatible.[4]

This challenge regarding the *Logos* was too dangerous to be avoided. However John had a secret weapon to counter the Pythagorean infiltration of Christianity and to ensure his readers knew his gospel was *not* a Gnostic treatise. The *Logos* represented all that was lovely—for everyone. However there was one number the Pythagorean Gnostics considered an abomination. Orthodox believers on the other hand so delighted in using this number, it could be considered the 'signature' of Christianity. John, naturally, opened his gospel with it.

---

[4] It would be easy to think that the divide between a belief in reincarnation and resurrection was a split on cultural lines: the Greeks leaning towards reincarnation and the Jews towards resurrection (though obviously, there were exceptions amongst the Jews, such as the Sadducees). But it was clearly not that simple. The question put to Jesus by His disciples concerning the blind man, '*Rabbi, who sinned, this man or his parents, that he was born blind?*' (John 9:2[BSB]) is thought to indicate a belief in the possibility of reincarnation that lingered from the days of the Babylonian exile.

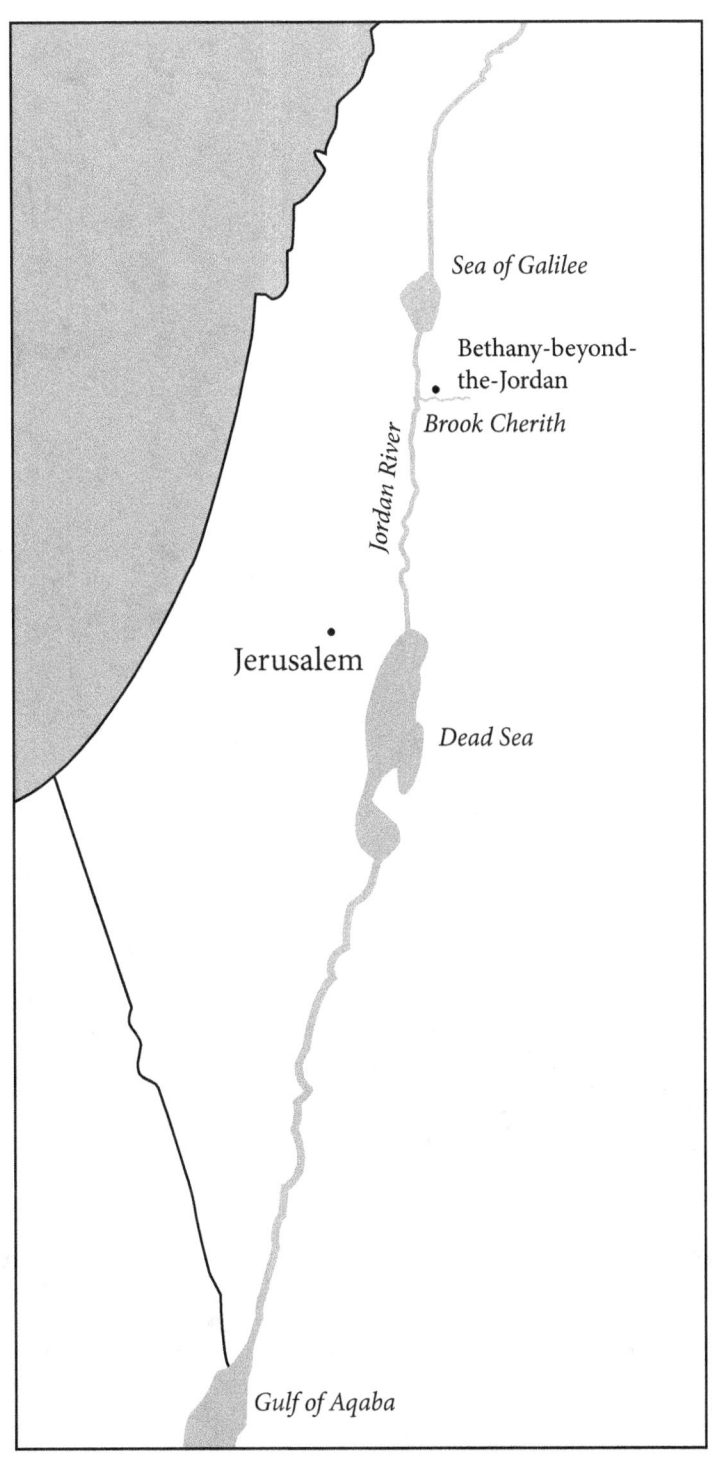

1.1 The Scribe

The fourth gospel is anonymous. Traditionally, of course, it has been credited to the apostle John. The Greek bishop, Irenaeus, writing in the second century, was the first to identify him as the author. Irenaeus also explained John's motives in setting down his testimony, thus outlining reasons for its strong contrast with the synoptic gospels.

Many commentators have doubts the apostle is the real author, based on the quality of the Greek and the sophistication of the theology. After all, John was a simple, illiterate fisherman from Galilee. This view of John as an ignorant manual worker has not moved on from the opinions of the Sanhedrin who grilled Peter and John after the healing of the man with crippled legs at the Beautiful Gate. These leaders were astonished that such 'unschooled, ordinary'[5] men were able to fling out Scripture quotations to boldly argue that Jesus was the Messiah.

For the Sanhedrin, anyone from Galilee was an uneducated rustic—so dismissing John the apostle as the author of this gospel today on the basis of those views is simply buying into first century prejudice. This bias is made worse by the scholarly assumption that John, over the best part of six decades of preaching and

---

5   Acts 4:13[NIV]

teaching, couldn't possibly develop a high literary style or a refined theology!

I personally believe that sufficient internal evidence points to John the apostle as the author. He didn't make it nearly as anonymous as it appears, particularly given its emphatic claims to eyewitness documentation.

According to Irenaeus, John wrote in opposition to the Nicolaitans and Gnostics, and also 'to remove that error which by Cerinthus had been disseminated among men.'[6] Cerinthus was a Jew from Egypt and one of the earliest Gnostics. He was known personally to the apostle John.

Irenaeus retold a story[7] about John going to the public baths in Ephesus. Suddenly becoming aware that Cerinthus was in the same building, John gathered his clothes and hurried out in case the wrath of God descended. 'Let us fly,' he cried, 'lest even the bath-house fall down, because Cerinthus, the enemy of the truth, is inside!'[8]

Cerinthus was a highly influential teacher whose doctrinal views became widespread across Asia Minor. He emerged about the year 88 and claimed that Jesus was not the Son of God but rather the biological child of Joseph and Mary. Allegedly, at His baptism, 'the Christ' descended on Jesus, giving Him miraculous powers. These remained until the time of the crucifixion when 'the Christ' departed from Him, leaving a mere human substitute to die on the cross. The anointed one, 'the Christ', was therefore a spirit untainted by death or corruption. Cerinthus also taught that

---

6   Irenaeus, Bishop of Lugdunum, *Against Heresies (Book III, Chapter 11)*, newadvent.org/fathers/0103311.htm (accessed 11 July 2021).

7   The story originally came from Irenaeus' teacher Polycarp.

8   jesuswalk.com/123john/stories-about-st-john.htm (accessed 11 July 2021)

Jesus would reign as the Messiah for one thousand years, through the power of the Logos coming on Him.[9]

It doesn't take any imagination to see that John, who had known Jesus—and who had lived and worked with Him, travelling up and down the dusty roads of Galilee, Samaria, Judea, Tyre, Sidon, the cities of the Decapolis beyond the Jordan, and the area around Caesarea Philippi—would have been intensely angered by this travesty of a story that presented Jesus as separate from 'the Christ'. John had been present at the crucifixion and yet somehow Cerinthus had become the 'expert' on the spiritual dynamics involved.

Concerned for truth to prevail, John prepared his gospel. His intention was to tell the real story of his beloved rabbi—Son of God, Son of Joseph—and to tell it in such a way no one could mistake the real spiritual dynamics.

Jesus had nicknamed John, along with his brother James, as 'Boanerges'—*sons of thunder*. John combined lightning and love in his proclamation of the gospel. There's grace and truth, but there's also a take-no-prisoners attitude in his writing. John knew the counterfeit teaching of his opponents and he took hold of it and flipped it right back against them.

John is thought to have been a teenager at the time he first began to follow Jesus. He was the son of Zebedee and the brother of James. His mother famously requested that her two sons would sit with Jesus, one on His right side, one on His left, when He

---

[9] biblegateway.com/resources/encyclopedia-of-the-bible/Cerinthus. Later Gnostics taught that the resurrection was a spiritual event, not a physical one. The promise of the resurrection for believers was understood in Gnostic thinking to be a release from the body, and essentially the same as dying. This contrasts with the early Christian view that Jesus was the First Fruits of those who would be raised from the dead and that resurrection meant that the physical body returned to life.

came into His kingdom. She is traditionally identified as Salome, who was present at the crucifixion.

Together with Peter and James, he made up the 'inner three' amongst the twelve disciples. They alone witnessed the raising of Jairus' daughter from the dead, the stunning glory of the Transfiguration and the agony of Jesus in the Garden of Gethsemane. John was tasked by Jesus with preparing the Passover meal. Later, at the crucifixion, he was commissioned to care for Jesus' mother. Alone of the twelve apostles, he heard Jesus' last words on the cross.

John was present with Peter at the tomb. He was also there when Peter was re-instated, during the breakfast on the shores of the Sea of Galilee. After the Ascension, he and Peter became prominent leaders of The Way. Irenaeus reported he eventually went to Ephesus, continuing the church founded there by Paul. This lasted until the time of the Emperor Trajan,[10] suggesting that John lived into his eighties. He would have been in his early seventies when the heresies of Cerinthus first began to gain traction and notoriety.

---

10   Trajan ruled from 98–117.

1.2 Numerical Literary Style

From at least the time of Plato during the fifth century before Christ, Greek literature adhered to classical ideals of elegance in form and structure. Language and number were combined together to define what Plato called the measure of the 'world soul'.[11]

Today we have digits for calculation that are separate from our alphabets but neither the Greek nor Hebrew civilisations had a similar format. Instead letters were assigned a numerical value and did double duty, performing a service in arithmetic as well as literature. An ancient poet would meticulously plan his epic by employing high-level mathematical skills we'd normally associate today with the fields of engineering, architecture, physics or astronomy. Creativity wasn't a free-for-all endeavour; it was disciplined and ordered, and writers were expected to conform to special tenets so that truth and beauty could bloom across their display.

Now this fusion of words and numbers was not confined to Greece by any means. It was widespread across the ancient world from Asia through the Middle East to Europe. Buddhist scriptures are said to be as much temples of mathematics as of words. The gospels and epistles can be described as wordscapes with embedded mathematical signs that blaze the way back up the trail into the Torah and Hebrew prophecy. This blended artform

---

11 See Robert Tavernor, *Smoot's Ear: The Measure of Humanity*, Yale University Press, 2007. In the *Timaeus*, Plato (427–347 BC) used Pythagoras' so-called perfect numbers as a means of describing the perfection of the natural harmony that existed in the world and universe. He did this by a synthesis of word and number he called the 'world soul'.

lasted for at least two and a half millennia, largely disappearing in western culture during the sixteenth century.[12] Throughout the medieval period, it resulted in poetry with stanzas that often seem unfinished or broken, but are simply structured according to the pattern of the *Logos*.

This is *not* numerology—which uses a number value assigned to each letter of the alphabet. That is entirely different.[13] The Greeks

---

[12] It's difficult to be sure why it vanished. Isolated poets still used it but, as a universal practice, it all but disappeared. If I were to venture a guess at the reasons, perhaps it was because in medieval times the *logos* marked truth, faith, fidelity and ultimate reality. Then, at the time of the Reformation, religious truth became a dangerously risky commodity. In England, the crown's expectation of religious loyalty violently see-sawed back and forth several times between Catholic and Protestant. Poets who wanted to preserve their lives had to become adept at hiding their own spiritual leanings behind slippery wordings. In such a volatile era, with truth the first casualty, the art of mathematical grammar associated with truth was therefore all but forgotten. (Anne Hamilton, *Gawain and the Four Daughters of God: the testimony of mathematics in Cotton Nero A.x,* Armour Books 2014)

[13] Amongst the techniques of numerology are the Greek practice of isopsephy (*equal pebbled* or *equal count*) and its Hebrew counterpart, gematria. Practitioners of isopsephy would:

(1) calculate the numerical value of a Greek word by adding the numbers associated with of each of the letters, and then

(2) correlate words with the same numerical value.

Exactly the same procedure was followed by practitioners of gematria using the Hebrew language. Words that shared the same numerical value were viewed as profoundly significant. 'Isopsephy can be viewed as an exegetical tool, a method of divination, and a theurgical technique.' (See isopsephy.com: *Cipher Mysticism in Greek Antiquity*)

The practice of gematria in Hebrew has come to be associated with the occult mysticism of the Kabbalah, however I am always mindful of the words of Ronald Youngblood: 'Flagrant abuse of various forms of numerology, including especially gematria, should not be permitted to blind us to the undoubted use of numbers in a figurative sense or of numbers as a literary device in the Bible (as well as elsewhere in the ancient world.)' While I have not looked extensively at the gematria of John's gospel, I am aware that he used it so I will be examining occasional numbers he repeatedly featured.

used the human body as their template of the ideal form and partitioned their works accordingly. Isocrates apologised to his readers, in one instance, for going outside the ideal canons of beauty to finish a story and, in another instance, for not finishing his account because he felt constrained to conform to the canons.

Numerical literary style is a term used by the Dutch theologians Joost Smit Sibinga and Maarten JJ Menken to describe the way scenes in the gospels are structured according to clearly defined arithmetic patterning.[14] Menken has analysed much of John's gospel and I will be calling on his expertise from time to time to show how the mathematical background enhances the text.

David Howlett describes these inbuilt structures as 'self-authenticating'. He makes the point that if, Patrick of Ireland sent out a pastoral epistle denouncing a Pictish king and this letter was to be disseminated by being copied and read in various Celtic churches, it was vital for the recipients to have some way of knowing they'd received the genuine words of the saint. Mathematical encoding was a way of providing a 'seal' for the text, given that offence to the local royals would have been a matter of life and death.

As early as the first century, the authentication of pastoral letters was already a crucial matter. In his second letter to the Thessalonians, Paul mentioned a forged epistle purporting to

---

14   This area of investigation is such a pioneering field that those who venture into it usually establish their own terminology. Besides Sibinga and Menken's 'numerical literary style', David Howlett uses the description 'Biblical style', Eleanor Bulatkin uses 'structural arithmetic metaphor', Donna Crawford 'architectonics', Maren-Sofie Røstvig 'arithmology' or 'arithmetic theology', Christiane Joost-Gaugier 'arithmology' or 'arithmosophy', Casper Labuschagne 'numerical compositions', Duane Christensen, 'logoprosodic analysis' (which combines musical and numerical investigations). In *Gawain and the Four Daughters of God*, an analysis of the four great medieval poems of the *Pearl* manuscript, I use the terms 'mathematical grammar' and 'mathematical tokens'.

have come from him to the effect that the 'Day of the Lord' had already arrived.[15] Internal mathematical elements would not necessarily have been a safeguard against fraudulent missives but they would have been a protection against corruption of the text.

The idea of guarding and preserving sacred texts against such degradation was regarded as so important within Jewish culture that an entire elite class arose, specifically devoted to this task. These highly educated men occasionally appear in the gospels, challenging Jesus. They were called the *sopherim*, the 'scribes'. That translation gives the impression they were *writers*, but their Hebrew name actually means the *counters*.[16] A scribe's three main tasks were:

(1) copy the Scriptures verbatim
(2) set the Scriptures in correct order
(3) count each letter, line, syllable, jot and tittle to ensure the text was duplicated exactly, word for word, so that not even the smallest missed stroke of the pen would happen or an element drop out of the Law.

The *sopherim* cross-checked manuscripts to testify to the truth of their transmission. Their mathematical 'proof-reading' provided independent verification of the copyist's work. Although their name, *counters*, gives the impression that all they had to do was add up, it wasn't actually that simple: the mathematical design of the text often incorporated special features such as square, rectangular, triangular and perfect numbers.[17]

This is why David Howlett suggests that this type of design 'self-authenticates' and 'seals' the text. The more complicated the design, the harder it is to tamper with, either deliberately or

---

15   2 Thessalonians 2:1–3
16   The name *Sopherim* comes from Hebrew 'caphar', *count, number, enumerate exactly* but also meaning *recount* or *talk*. Names such as Joseph, *God adds*, are related to it.

accidentally. In the days before photocopies and scanners, it was crucial to have internal verification of the message.[18]

---

17   Hebrew *Sopherim* of the fourth century were said to be so concerned with getting the count right with regard to each jot and tittle of the Torah that they argued whether the middle letter and middle verse belonged to its first or second half. (MJJ Menken, *Numerical Literary Techniques in John – The Fourth Evangelist's Use of Numbers of Words and Syllables*, Supplements to Novum Testamentum, Vol LV, E.J. Brill, 1985) Menken's analysis of the letter, word, syllable and sentence count of much of John's gospel allowed him to reach the conclusion that the numerical design underlying the scene structures is so tightly controlled that, at most, a single syllable *may* have been lost across two millennia.

By the fifth century, the traditions of the *Sopherim* were beginning to be codified by the Masoretes. By the end of the first millennium, in the early Middle Ages, these scribes had started to include additional elements within the scrolls. Because of their concerns that traditions, including pronunciation of words, were in danger of being lost, these elements included vocalization aids (vowel points), accentuation (musical signs) and the 'masorah', an apparatus of instructions which included notes on how to write the letters, statistics on word frequency and textual references. (See thetorah.com/article/the-bible-and-the-masoretic-text, accessed 28 November 2021)

The Masoretic Text is now the standard for use in Jewish communities throughout the world. Its name is said to come from 'masoreth', *tradition*. Grant Jeffrey suggests that 'Masorete' comes from the Hebrew word for *fence* or *wall* which refers to their extreme care of the scribes in copying the text. They were creating a 'fence around the Law' to defend its absolute accuracy. For example, out of the 78,064 Hebrew letters in Genesis, the Masoretes counted 8448 'yod' letters. A master examiner would scrutinise a completed scroll and, if any error was found, the manuscript was destroyed to prevent it being copied and transmitting an error. (Grant R Jeffrey, *The Signature of God: Astonishing Biblical Discoveries*, Tyndale House Publishers 1997, p14.)

In earlier times, however, during the era when the Temple still operated, professional correctors were employed to safeguard the precision of the text. These specialists were paid out of the Temple funds. (thetorah.com/article/the-scribes-of-proto-mt-and-their-practices, accessed 28 November 2021)

18   My apologies to those who have a phobia about mathematics but I find the idea of combining words and numbers irresistible. Ever since I learned of the technique, I've employed it in my writing. The first three sections in this book, for example, are 888 words long because 888 is a number associated with the name Jesus in Greek.

For the gospels and epistles, this 'self-authentication' combined with an element important to Greek literature: the idea of textual beauty in terms of its mathematical design.[19] The very mention of the Logos would have primed a Greek reader to expect an overall architecture based on the proportions of an idealised human male.

But John didn't bow to the canons of Greek poetry. Instead, he looked straight to the sacred Scriptures of his own people for inspiration regarding the grand overarching design of his gospel. And from the poetry of the prophets He chose a technique called *chiasmus*.

---

19   MJJ Menken, *Numerical Literary Techniques in John – The Fourth Evangelist's Use of Numbers of Words and Syllables*, quoting Karl Menninger, *Zahlwort und Ziffer, Eine Kulturgeschichte der Zahl*, Göttingen, 1979

1.3 Poetry of the Prophets

Hebrew poetry is as different from modern free verse as medieval alliterative forms are from sonnets with their rhyming couplets.

Although rhyme is sometimes a significant aspect of Hebrew poetry, it tends to be head-rhyme, rather than tail-rhyme—and that means the beginnings of words rhyme, rather than the endings. Puns and words with double or triple meanings add a rich textural underlay to any poetic scheme. Although translators tend to opt for just one out of these multiplicity of meanings—usually the traditional one—it often seems the prophet chose particular words precisely because they resonated in a variety of ways. Modern education trains us to look for singular definitions and specific meanings, but the wordplay suggests a wide vista of possibilities. In the case of double meanings, it's not necessarily a choice between two options—sometimes there's a sense we are meant to choose both!

Rhyme, however, is not the most prominent or common feature of Hebrew poetry. Its distinctive character can perhaps best be seen in the themed echoes or doublets of ideas found throughout so many prophecies. When these are expanded beyond a verse or two, the symmetrical, mirrored form known as 'chiasmus' emerges.

Chiasmus is similar to palindromes—words or numbers that read the same backwards as forwards. Consider:

- Never odd or even.
- Was it a car or a cat I saw?
- 1743471
- Saippuakivikauppias

The last is the longest word palindrome in everyday use. It's Finnish for a person who sells soapstone.[20]

Chiasmus is defined as a *rhetorical or literary device in which words, grammatical constructions, or concepts are repeated in reverse order.* An example[21] can be found in Isaiah 28, from which this tiny snippet is taken:

> [15] **For you said, 'We have made a <u>covenant with death</u>; we have fashioned an AGREEMENT WITH SHEOL. When the** *overwhelming scourge* **passes through it will not touch us, because we have made lies our refuge and falsehood our hiding place.'**
>
> > [16] *So this is what the Lord God says: 'See, I lay a stone in Zion, a tested stone, a precious cornerstone, a sure foundation; the one who believes will never be shaken.* [17a] *I will make justice the measuring line and righteousness the level.*
>
> [17b] **Hail will sweep away your refuge of lies, and water will flood your hiding place.** [18] **Your <u>covenant with death</u> will be dissolved, and your AGREEMENT WITH SHEOL will not stand. When the** *overwhelming scourge* **passes through, you will be trampled by it.**[22]

---

20 And it's appropriate to mention this here, since soapstone actually appears in the second chapter of John's gospel. See the next volume in this series.

21 Another example is found in Mark's gospel from chapter 6 verse 30 through to chapter 8 verse 11 which begins with Jesus feeding five thousand and ends with Him feeding four thousand.

22 Emphasis added throughout to indicate patterning.

This extract shows the central summit of Isaiah's poem in verses 16 and 17ᵃ and the chiastic ideas evident in the parallel between verses 15 and 17ᵇ–18, which both[23] mention five elements:

- a covenant with Death
- an agreement with Sheol
- a refuge of lies
- falsehood as a hiding place
- an overwhelming scourge

This is the part of Isaiah's poem where the symmetry of ideas is so plain it's unmistakable. In the verses before and after this tiny segment, the historical allusions are so dense, it's hard to penetrate the parallelism. The same is true in John's gospel: there are sections so blatant they are difficult to miss but then the symbolism becomes so subtle and dense it's difficult to recognise and be able to pair up the matching themes.

This book began in a strange way. I was writing an article and I wanted to quote a scholar who had remarked that the identification of the writer of the gospel at the end was positioned in a way to mirror the naming of John the Baptiser at the beginning. Unfortunately I couldn't remember which scholar it was or what book it was in. My initial efforts on the internet, while fruitless in terms of my own search, turned up lots of small lists of two or three items that appeared at the beginning as well as the end of John's gospel. None of these listings were the same, so I started to collate them. Very quickly, once I'd got the idea, I started to add items myself.

---

23   If you're asking yourself why the verses don't match perfectly and have to be split to show the correspondences, it's important to remember that our present verse numbering didn't exist for over two millennia after Isaiah spoke forth this prophecy. Chapter divisions were only introduced in the twelfth century, while the sub-division into verses happened in the sixteenth century.

It was incredibly easy at first. It seemed clear that John, in order to pave the way for Gentiles like me to catch on to the overall design, had arranged it so that people who had the same names appeared in the chiastic scenes. The mother of Jesus appeared at the start—paralleling Mary Magdalene at the end. Nicodemus turned up front and back. Nathanael, only mentioned twice in all Scripture, was mentioned in a similar fashion. Each of these paired scenes not only had people with the same name but they also had the same theme.

Eventually, it seemed John gave up the chiastic idea and headed off to mention the signs Jesus performed, thereby satisfying the Jewish desire for the miraculous, as well as keeping Greeks happy with various fine examples of Christ's wisdom. The parallelism broke down, in my view, because there was nothing in common between Jesus meeting the woman of Samaria and Jesus facing Pilate. This faulty opinion persisted for several months until it finally dawned on me that both scenes were about *kingship*. The parallelism of names had gone, but the themes had not.

So where's the centre of John's gospel? Where's the summit? I believe it is the double peak in John 10 where Jesus says, 'I am the Good Shepherd,' and later, 'I am the Gate of the Sheep.'

If you were wondering why this first volume concentrates on John 1 and John 21, this is the reason. It's so we can look at what the chiasmus reveals to us. I'd like to make one last remark on this Hebrew form and, although it is speculative in nature, I think it is worth considering. Plato in *Theaetetus* quoted the philosopher Protagoras: 'Man is the measure of all things.' That sentiment very much sums up the way Greek literature was designed. Just as the architecture of the Parthenon included the golden ratio because it dominated the proportions of the ideal human form in classical thinking, so too was Greek poetry framed around this mathematical touchstone.

However, for the Hebrews, it was entirely different. Permit me to put on my teacher-of-mathematics hat for just a moment. I promise to take it off by the end of the paragraph. A ratio is *not* a number in and of itself. Strictly speaking, the golden ratio is *not* approximated as 0.618, despite what you may have read in *The Da Vinci Code*. Actually, it would more correct to say it's about 0.618 *to 1*. This is important because a ratio actually describes a *relationship*, not a number in its own right. All ratios are properly expressions that show the proportional relationship between two lengths or two areas or two volumes. In fact, ratios are not restricted to two of anything. The quantities given in recipes, for example, are really proportions ideal for home baking. They can be halved or doubled or tripled or multiplied by a hundred or a thousand—and, in each case, the ratios of the ingredients, one to another, would remain the same.

While the Greeks concentrated on *measure*, the Hebrews made a subtle distinction and focused on *relationship*. For them, *relationship* was primarily expressed through *covenant*. And covenant is why I suspect chiasmus is framed in mirror pairs, symmetrically arranged.

To raise a blood covenant, an animal was cut in two.[24] The divided parts were placed a short distance away from each other with a gap where a pool of blood collected. The participants would walk in a figure-of-eight through the pool of blood and stand between the divided parts to recite their vows. These included blessings and curses.

The curse basically went along these lines: *if I violate this covenant may I die just as this animal has died.*

---

24 The technical terms for making a covenant were 'to raise' (when it was with God) or 'to cut' (with anyone).

And the blessing, whatever the wording, fundamentally said: *I will give my life for you if necessary, just as this animal gave its life.*

The symmetry of the covenant ceremony is, I believe, the reason for the symmetry of the chiastic poetic form. The use of it as the immense overarching architecture of John's gospel is therefore not simply a cultural preference on the writer's part, it speaks to the most profound theological deeps that separate the Greek and Hebrew worlds. In the Greek cosmos, the best you could ever hope for was to appease the gods. In the Hebrew you could, through the atonement of covenant, become friends with the Lord of all creation.

1.4 The Mirror Summarised

The design of John's gospel is simply exquisite—it uses matching themes in a mirrored arrangement, rather than a chronological approach. This is not to say that it is never sequential, because there definitely are occasions when it clearly states *'the next day'*, *'the following day'* or *'three days later'*. However, when it doesn't give a time reference, it is unwise to assume one. When scholars have presumed a linear progression of events in John's gospel, then it follows that particular incidents were duplicated during the ministry of Jesus. This includes episodes like clearing the moneychangers out of the Temple and the invitation to dinner that was interrupted by a woman who anointed His feet with oil.

However, once it's obvious that the design is chiastic and based around matching thematic elements, it's a different story. Technically, 'chiasmus' is defined as a *rhetorical or literary device in which words, grammatical constructions, or concepts are repeated in reverse order.* This is precisely the nature of the pattern John used: his writing works inwards from both back and front simultaneously. I believe that the summit of his gospel is a double peak: it culminates in a central doublet with two 'I Am' statements and a shepherd motif. These two statements are: 'I Am the Good Shepherd' and 'I Am the Gate of the sheep.' This is the point in the gospel when the themes start to reverse.

The following summary skates across the surface of John's pattern. Each matching pair has deep internal links and also, in many cases, with the episodes on either side of them. John emphasises two aspects of the Christ in his presentation: the Shepherd and the Bridegroom.

His gospel starts with several significant numerical features which are mirrored in the final chapter, before he launches into the testimony of a man named John. At the start, John the Baptiser speaks of the Lamb of God and, at the end, the disciple Jesus loved records Jesus' instructions about lambs and sheep.

Next the gospel tells of five disciples, including Simon Peter and Nathanael, who go after Jesus into Galilee. And, similarly positioned at the end, five groups of disciples, again including Simon Peter and Nathanael, head off after Jesus into Galilee. Nathanael is only ever mentioned in Scripture in these two places.

Embedded in the gathering of disciples for this first trip is a brief story about Nathanael having doubts. Matching this at the end is the episode of Thomas having doubts. This is one of the few places in the first half dozen pairs where the names don't match—however, if we assume the accuracy of the long Christian tradition that Bartholomew and Nathanael are the same person, then the match is very much closer since both Thomas and Bartholomew are derived from the name Ptolemy.[25] Thus John seems to have included the Nathanael-has-doubts story, assuming that his readers knew Nathanael was also called Bartholomew, *son of Ptolemy*.

Moving on from these occasions, there are matching incidents with two women named Mary. At the beginning, the woman is the mother of Jesus. At the end, it's Mary Magdalene. In both cases, the conversation is about bridal issues—at the start, it's about the

---

25   In turn, Ptolemy is believed to be derived from 'Tolmai'.

provision of wine for the wedding feast at Cana and, at the end, the dialogue between Jesus and Mary Magdalene in the garden outside the tomb reflects the bridal scene in the *Song of Songs*.

Far be it from us, however, to deduce from this that Mary was married to Jesus—as many have done. The couplet of stories involving Nicodemus puts paid to that notion.

After this in John's narrative, the time sequence breaks down. Instead, the thematic pattern emerges more fully. The paired stories are Jesus overturning the tables of the money-changers and emptying the Temple with the account of the tomb being discovered empty. Because of the placement right after the Cana story, some scholars think that John's description of the ousted money-changers refers to an incident early in Jesus' career. They regard the story told by Matthew and Mark as describing a similar, but separate, and very much later event. However, John puts no time frame on the incident, apart from mentioning that it occurred near the Passover. Up to this point in his narrative his dating was very clear. *'The next day,'* he says in both John 1:35 and 1:43 and *'on the third day'* in John 2:1. No such time-stamp appears on the story of emptying the Temple. I think the specific mention of the Passover is the first clue to look for theme, rather than timing.

It's clear to me this incident did not happen twice. John describes one-and-the-same event as Matthew and Mark, however he positioned it with the intention of forming a literary pair with the empty tomb. The thematic link between Temple and tomb would have been evident to his readers—they would have known a sacred shekel had an image of the godling of death on it. The priestly hierarchy, prohibited from minting their own coins by the Romans, chose to get the highest quality silver from Tyre—and insisted the Temple tax could only be paid using these foreign-made shekels with a pagan godling on them. The money-changers charged exorbitant fees to trade this offensive currency for ordinary coins. So John's point in matching these two scenes is: just as Jesus drove the godling of death from the Temple, so too He drove it from the tomb.

The next set of paired stories in the line-up involve Nicodemus. In the first episode, Jesus states it's necessary to be 'born again of water and the Spirit.' The meaning of this enigmatic phrase is only apparent in the parallel episode when Nicodemus is present at the crucifixion and sees the soldier pierce Jesus' side with a lance. Observing blood and water flow and knowing that the Greek word for 'blood' in this instance also means 'spirit', he would have realised that this was the moment of new birth. Just as the first Adam's bride, Eve, was born from his side, the Bride of Christ had just been birthed from the side of the Second Adam.

And then we're back to the two Johns. At the beginning, the Baptiser is testifying of the Bridegroom and at the end the Apostle is testifying of the last words of Jesus: *'It is finished!'* In Hebrew, this is 'kalah' which also means *my bride* and has the overtones: 'It is consummated!'[26]

The next set of story pairs involves Jesus meeting the Samaritan woman and Jesus before Pilate. At this point, the name matching breaks down and only the deep themes remain in play. Both these stories feature truth, water and kingship. Indeed when it comes right down to it, they're about the proclamation of the true king.

And so the pairs go on and on. Until they hit a snag. And if there was going to be a hitch, there was one obvious place for it: the start of John chapter 8. This is the story of the woman caught in adultery. Some ancient manuscripts don't include this story at all;

---

26 Footnote to John 19:30 in Brian Simmons, *John: Eternal Love, The Passion Translation*, Broadstreet Publishing Group, Wisconsin 2014

some include it, in whole or in part, after John 7:36, John 21:25, Luke 21:38 or Luke 24:53.

Ivan Panin pointed out that this is one of only two passages of any substantial length in the four gospels that are disputed. The earliest manuscript copies we have do not include the last twelve verses of Mark or this scene from John's gospel. Common to both the end of Mark and the story of the woman caught in adultery is God's grace to less-than-virtuous women. In the first, Mary Magdalene—notorious as the person who had seven demons cast out of her by Jesus—is honoured by being recorded as the first witness of the resurrection. In the second, a woman caught in the middle of a sexual liaison with a married man is presented to Jesus. Instead of condemning her, He writes on the ground, in some mysterious way shaming her accusers. Once they have left, He offers her forgiveness and a second chance.

Panin has noted that, at least in the case of Mark's gospel, while our earliest *copies* lack the last twelve verses, *even* earlier writings refer to them. He suggested that some copyist, like Uzzah who reached out his hand to steady the Ark of the Covenant, felt the need to 'right' the testimony of the apostles when it came to the place of women.[27]

Is there any way we can know where this story rightly goes? Luke or John? And, if John, does the patterning suggest a proper placement? I believe this story does indeed belong in John and that it's possible to know where it was first located. Instead of the beginning of chapter 8, I believe it should come at the end of that chapter—after the dispute between Jesus and the Pharisees about His identity.

---

[27] Ivan Panin's magisterial mathematical analysis of these verses includes a comparison with the opening verses of the same gospel, showing both have the same 'numerical signature'.

If that happens, then in my opinion, all the paired episodes line up beautifully.

The story of the woman caught in adultery then matches Mary of Bethany anointing Jesus' head with oil and washing His feet with her tears. There's a very strong hint they are the same person. Or, if not, their sins are much the same. And that might suggest the removal of these two stories from early manuscripts was not about excising the role of women from the record but censoring the role of one particular woman: Mary Magdalene.

Yet that would be to defy a prophecy of Jesus as the freshly anointed king who, on the following day, was to ride into Jerusalem to be acclaimed by the people.

PART

In the Beginning was the Word,
and the Word was with God
and the Word was God.
The same was
in the beginning with God.
All things were made by Him;
and without Him
was not anything made
that was made.

John 1:1-3 KJV

TWO

There are many more things
that Jesus did.
If all of them were
written down,
I suppose that not even
the world itself
would have space
for all the books
that would be written.

John 21:25 BSB

2.1 Poet and Poem

In the beginning was the Word, and the Word was with God, and the Word was God. The same was in the beginning with God. All things were made by Him; and without Him was not any thing made that was made.

John 1:1–3^{KJV}

*There are many more things that Jesus **did**. If all of them were written down, I suppose that not even the world itself would have space for the books that would be written.*

John 21:25^{BSB}

In his opening, John refers to Jesus as the Word who made the world. At the very end he comments that the world would not be sufficient to contain the books necessary to describe the deeds—the *poetry*—of His life.

Perhaps it seems that, in describing the work of Jesus as 'poetry', I've taken a deep dive into the dreamy rose-coloured fog of romanticism. Yet it's not mystic at all. In fact, it's unashamedly literal. That deceptively simple rendering, 'There are many more things that Jesus did,' conceals His identity as the divine Poet.

In the original Greek, the word for *did* comes from 'poieō', *to make* or *to do*. It's the source of the English word *poem*. So when words and books are under discussion, 'poieó' means *to compose a poem*.

He is not only the Word who spoke the cosmos into existence through the power of His breath, He is the Poet who continues to redeem it through the power of His blood.

Ephesians 2:10[NKJV] informs us, *'We are His workmanship, created in Christ Jesus for good works, which God prepared beforehand that we should walk in them.'* That word, *workmanship*, is also derived from 'poieó', *to make* or *to do*, and again refers to *poetry*. We are God's poetry! And we are created by the Master Poet, Jesus of Nazareth, to walk out that poetry in our lives and to partner with Him in a lyric of restoration.

> *'We are God's fellow workers. You are God's field, God's building.'*
>
> 1 Corinthians 3:9[ESV]

Here we are reminded that God calls us to collaborate with Him and bring to fruition His purposes in our lives for the world around us.

> *'The whole creation is on tiptoe to see the wonderful sight of the sons of God coming into their own.'*
>
> Romans 8:19[PHPS]

Ken Bailey spent forty years in the Middle East, immersed in both the culture and language. He indicated it would have been very easy for the gospel writers to have recalled the words of Jesus even decades later because, when rendered back into Aramaic, it's clear some sayings were incredibly memorable poems. We often forget that the epistles and most of the gospels were composed in Greek by disciples who thought in Aramaic. In a very real sense then, these works—even as they were first set down—were *already* translations. It's arguable whether poetry or humour is the first casualty of translation but, either way, they both fall off a cliff in our modern English versions.

We're not used to thinking of Jesus as a brilliant poet. Bailey, however, comments on the exquisite, intricate, technically dazzling and irresistibly playful reconstructions he knew of, as 'the work of a skilled… poet in the first century. There remains no reason to doubt that the author was Jesus of Nazareth.'[28]

Would John, the beloved disciple, have tried to emulate Jesus in the crafting of words? The answer, I believe, is self-evident.

---

28 Kenneth Bailey, *Poet and Peasant: A Literary-Cultural Approach to the Parables in Luke*, William B. Eerdmans Publishing Co., 1983

2.2 The Cosmic Canticle

In the beginning was the Word, and the Word was with God, and the Word was God.

John 1:1^{ESV}

Not even the world itself would have space for the books that would be written.

John 21:25^{BSB}

'In the beginning...' This deliberate invocation of the opening words of Genesis begins what some commentators have called the *Hymn to the Logos*. This suggests that John did not limit himself to the creation of a poem, but envisaged his gospel as a song.

His canticle of praise recalls the anthem that greeted the dawn of creation when *'the morning stars sang together and all the sons of God shouted for joy.'* (Job 38:7^{BSB})

Intuitively, after the words, *'In the beginning...'* we expect to see: *'...God created the heavens and the earth.'* John reframes those heart-stirring words to point first and foremost to the Word incarnate. Yet, because this is a chiastic[29] structure—the first verse of the gospel both informing and being informed by the last verse of the gospel—we should examine the impact of the final words.

---

29   A chiasmus is a poetic arrangement as discussed in section 1.3. His gospel is arranged in symmetrical scenes and thoughts. In some cases, there is broad symmetry while in others the parallelism is fine and detailed.

Brian Simmons notes that the Aramaic version[30] of this last line says: *'The world itself would be emptied out into the books that would be written.'*[31]

The original Greek word here for *world* is 'kosmos'. While *world* is not inaccurate, 'kosmos' has further nuances of *universe, cosmos, the entirety of creation*. That puts a whole new spin on what John was saying: *creation itself is not sufficient to contain a record of the deeds—the poetry—performed by Jesus of Nazareth.*

This wondrous statement reveals the relationship between the Creator and His creation. Although He came into it, it cannot contain Him. It can't even contain the stories about Him! He emptied Himself to become nothing in order to fit into the vessel of creation, yet still He overflows it.

In a later age, the shades of meaning behind 'kosmos' came to greatly influence the medieval imagination. The word 'kosmos' is derived from *ornament*, so in the Middle Ages, people conceived of the universe as a jeweled brooch worn on God's breast, close to His heart.

'The universe is made of stories, not of atoms,' wrote Muriel Rukeyser. Perhaps that seems too unscientific for this present age, yet we are assured by physicists that our apparently solid, material world is basically composed of vibrations. Surely songs and speech are also vibrations: patterned vibrations, of course, but isn't pattern the imposition of order on chaos?

John's opening and closing words are crammed full of weighty glory. His beginning primes the reader to transport all the

---

30 The oldest Aramaic version of the gospels and epistles that we have, the Peshitta, dates from the fifth century. The oldest Greek versions at present date from the fourth century.

31 Footnote to John 21:25 in Brian Simmons, *John: Eternal Love, The Passion Translation*, Broadstreet Publishing Group, Wisconsin 2014.

familiarity and wonder they associate with the creation story across into their understanding of Jesus. John's set-up means no one will ever read the first verse of Genesis again without being reminded, even if it's unconsciously, that the Wordsmith who created the heavens and the earth is Jesus of Nazareth.

2.3 'Unnecessary' Words

*In the beginning was the Word, and the Word was **with** God, and the Word was God.*

John 1:1[ESV]

*And there are also many other things that Jesus did, which if they were written one by one, I suppose that even the world itself could not contain the books that would be written. **Amen.***

John 21:25[NKJV]

THE VERY LAST WORD OF JOHN's gospel varies according to the translation you prefer. Some versions have *amen* and some don't.[32] It all depends on the particular manuscript the translators decided to work from. Almost all of the more recent translations have chosen to leave *amen* out.

The omission doesn't detract from the actual gospel storyline, so we may in some ways consider amen to be an 'unnecessary' finale. It does, however, have an impact on the word and letter count—and while that's totally irrelevant to us, it certainly wasn't to the readers of the first century.[33]

---

32 Some even have the following words at the end: '*the Gospel according to John was given out thirty-two years after the ascension of Christ*.' John Gill indicates that this would date the gospel to the year 66, before the war with the Romans and the destruction of the Temple. Most commentators, however, place the composition of the work just before the end of the first century.

33 With the *amen*, there are 25 words, 112 letters and a gematria of 9156. Without the *amen*, there are 24 words, 108 letters and a gematria of 9057.

More importantly, a final *amen* attests to the truth of John's account. He has set a seal on his writing as the testimony of a true and faithful witness. *Amen* has the sense of *truly* as well as *so let it be*. It is derived from the Hebrew word 'aman', meaning *confirm, be firm, support, establish, be steadfast*.

It also points back, yet again, to the opening words of Genesis:

> *In the beginning God created the heavens and the earth.*
>
> Genesis 1:1[NKJV]

Transliterated from Hebrew, these seven words are: *bereshit bara Elohim* **et** *hashamayim ve'et ha'arets*. In the middle of this sentence is '**et**', the fourth word. I've emphasised it in bold. It's never translated. So, in some respects, it might be considered 'unnecessary'.

There's an incommensurable chasm between the extremes of Jewish mysticism and Christian rationalism. And that gulf is nowhere better shown up as in their respective teachings about this 'non-translatable' word. Hebrew language courses at almost all universities and colleges with a western heritage present '**et**' as little more than a grammatical point. It's considered simply to be a marker that indicates the following word is either in the accusative case or is the definite direct object.

This dry, dessicating explanation jettisons the rabbinical viewpoint[34] on this mysterious word—one important enough to appear as the fourth word of all Scripture. The barren nature of this definition of '**et**' indicates just how deep the inroads of

---

34 Avram Yehoshua rightly points out the dangers of kabbalistic thought in some rabbinical commentaries about 'et'—ideas that, if pursued, may draw readers towards a study of the occult. There is no wisdom in the extreme opposite, however, since that eventually leads into the equally perilous territory of either replacement theology or gnosticism.

mechanistic intellectualism sometimes are. Ideology has often replaced theology. Comprised of alef and tav, the first and last letters of the Hebrew alphabet, 'et' is a combination just like alpha-omega, the first and last letters of the Greek alphabet.

Orthodox Jewish scholars of a more mystical bent therefore maintain that 'et' symbolises both the alphabet as a whole and, in addition, all possible combinations of letters within it. Thus, alef-tav represents every possible and conceivable word.

Furthermore the positioning of alef-tav immediately preceding 'hashamayim', *the heavens*—the first created thing—is also seen as highly significant. It tells us that words herald the act of creation. They also describe the method of creation. Furthermore they form the vessel of creation and consequently cast the shape of it. In addition, they are qualified to be true witnesses to it.

Herald – Method – Vessel – Shape – Witness

This fivefold aspect of alef-tav is a sublimely beautiful and poetic contrast to the thought that it is merely a point of grammar. Because the Greek equivalent of alef-tav is alpha-omega, messianic Jewish believers often see alef-tav as a reference to Jesus, the Word who was God and who was with God and who, pre-eminent above creation, existed before the foundation of the world. After all, He is both the First and the Last, the Alpha and Omega.

> '*I am the Alpha and the Omega,*' says the Lord God, '*who is, and who was, and who is to come, the Almighty.*'
>
> Revelation 1:8^{NIV}

The qualification of alef-tav as a witness to creation comes from the understanding that, first, words and letters are living beings and, secondly, the testimony of two witnesses is the minimum requirement under the Law. Alef-tav might simply be, whenever it appears in the Hebrew Scriptures—all 11,050 times—shorthand for 'this is true' or *truly*.³⁵

It would therefore perform substantially the same function as *amen* in the gospels and epistles. You can leave out *truly* and it makes no difference to the story. Like *amen*, '**et**' is not strictly necessary to an understanding of the text.

Avram Yehoshua—who differs considerably from the views I've expressed above—points out that '**et**' is *not* always *un*translatable.³⁶ It sometimes means *ploughshare* and it sometimes means *you* in the feminine singular, that is, when *you* refers to a woman by herself. In addition, it sometimes means *with*. In this respect, it's controversially been used in the Hebrew text of John 1:1—*and the Word was **with** God*.

Not every scholar agrees with this usage and modern Hebrew translations have dropped it. It's by no means easy to find a balance between a desire for technical accuracy and apportioning due measure to any lyrical impulse. Yet Scripture is often poetry, playing with evocative phrasings and subtle allusions from multiple sources. This lack of balance pervades both scholarly analysis of the text as well as scientific denial of the record. Now I certainly won't suggest science agrees with this idea of words preceding creation, but it certainly doesn't disagree. Current scientific theory suggests that the universe came into being through vibrations, like sound. Now is that sound merely random

---

35 I used to become disappointed when numbers like 11,050 appeared. Why couldn't it be 11,111—a number so full of, and fulfilling, covenant imagery that it is like the breath of God across Scripture? Well, I've learned better. 11,050 is divisible by 50 (the number of Jubilee), by 17 (the number of Christianity and a reference to the original name of God) and 13 (the number of 'threshold').

36 It hardly seems right to quote someone in support of a viewpoint he'd disagree with, so in fairness I'm pointing out that this is the case. If you'd like to consult his perspective, see seedofabraham.net/jat.htm

noise or is it patterned in some way and therefore encoded with meaning? And is there any essential difference, realistically speaking, between a sound encoded with meaning and a word?

2.4 The Golden Ratio

*In the beginning was the **Word**, and the **Word** was with God, and the **Word** was God.*

John 1:1^{NIV}

*If all of them were **written** down, I suppose that not even the world itself would have space for the books that would be **written**.*

John 21:25^{BSB}

Word, Word, Word. Logos: in the first verse the *Word*, the *Reason* and the *Ratio* are mentioned three times.

Written, written… and, in the second last[37] verse, *written*. Again three times—indicating the Word is an active principle, not a passive abstraction. The divine parable-maker and poet who sings over His beloved has entered the world, not remained aloof from it. He is the Logos—the *Word*, the *Reason* and the *Ratio*—and He is ideal, but not in the way the world ever anticipated. That's the thrust of John's coupling of *Word* and *written*.

In the first century the *Logos* was a term with a thick underlay of Platonic and Pythagorean philosophy. So its intended meaning couldn't be left, hopefully hidden, under the carpet. It would

---

37 Again, it's important to remember not to pay too much attention to verse divisions that were created well over fourteen centuries after the completion of the text.

have been all too easy for Gentiles to get the wrong idea if the subject was avoided. There was far more at stake than a religious distinction between the humanistic 'measure of man' and covenantal relationship with heaven. The issue of its provenance had to be addressed—not least because John needed to establish the identity of the Creator from the outset. The Logos would have been an ambiguous term for many Greek readers, instantly bringing to mind Pythagoras and Python Apollo. That notion needed to be dispelled as quickly as possible.

Python Apollo was the tutelary deity of the oracle at Delphi. Pythagoras was named after this particular manifestation of Apollo. He was a philosopher who established a religion of numbers—classifying odd numbers as male and 'good', and even numbers as female and 'evil'. He thereby did more to entrench misogyny—hatred of women—in western civilisation than perhaps any other individual. This was probably an unintentional outcome of his system. However, when combined with the natural disposition of the ancient Greek male to despise women, it became such a pervasive mindset that Scriptural interpretation has bowed before it, rather than the opposite.

Menander cursed the hero Prometheus for creating the 'foul tribe of women' and Hesiod describes females as having 'a bitch's mind and deceptive character... lies and wily words.' Women were considered a 'sheer trap', a 'plague'. Semonides classed them as 'the greatest evil', Aristotle as 'irrational' and 'mutilated'. Socrates began each morning by thanking the gods he was not born a woman.[38]

The enduring legacy of Pythagoras has been to legitimise the view that the world of the patriarchs marginalised women—when,

---

38   Bruce S Thornton, *Eros: The Myth Of Ancient Greek Sexuality*, Routledge 1997

in fact, it often celebrated them as pioneers and trail-blazers.[39] Jewish commentaries on the role of women in the Exodus are stunningly different from the usual Christian exegesis, portraying the mothers of Israel with such exceptional honour that it's a shock to encounter this viewpoint for the first time.[40] The general view of women in the church has vastly more to do with the doctrines of Pythagoras than with the teaching of Jesus.[41]

The Pythagorean Brotherhood managed to attach their founder's name to the famous theorem about right triangles that you probably learned in high school. Yet he was not its discoverer. He was in fact taught how to solve quadratic equations by the magi.

When he was studying in Egypt, the Persian armies invaded and took him off as a captive to Babylon which they'd conquered half a dozen years beforehand. There he was assigned work with the magi and was taught their mathematical lore. Given the

---

[39] Who was the first person to praise God? Who was the first to give Him a name? Who was the first to announce the coming of God's Messiah? Who was Paul's mentor and coach? Who financed Jesus' ministry? Who anointed Him king? Who saved the life of Moses when he was a baby and later left her royal position to marry an Israelite? Who was the first Hebrew to build a city in Canaan? The answers: Leah, Hagar, Hannah, Phoebe, Joanna, Mary Magdalene, Bithiah and Sheerah, the granddaughter of Joseph. The names of all these women and their actions are set down in Scripture.

[40] My reaction on first coming across these observations was reeling disbelief. Surely, I thought, in all my reading I'd have long ago come to know that the women of the Exodus refused to give any of their jewelry for the fashioning of the golden calf. And that, on the contrary, they were the first to offer their ornaments for the adornment of the Tabernacle. How could it possibly be that they were the first to accept the Law at Mount Sinai? Did the Bible really say that? If it did, how could it have become so hidden? These questions got me started but they barely scratch the surface of the role of women in Scripture and the esteem they were accorded. See: *More Precious than Pearls* and *As Resplendent as Rubies* and *As Exceptional as Sapphires*, all part of the series, *The Mother's Blessing and God's Favour Towards Women*.

[41] For a secular take on the ongoing influence of Pythagoras regarding science, religion and the place of women, see: Margaret Wertheim, *Pythagoras's Trousers: God, Physics, and the Gender War*, W.W. Norton Company 1997.

dates, he apparently just missed meeting and studying under the prophet Daniel.

According to the book that bears his name, Daniel was twice appointed chief of the magi. He knew their mathematical secrets inside out. However, just a few years previously, after the fall of the Babylonian empire, he'd been whisked off east to serve the king of Persia. There he again rose to prominence, in yet another foreign land. It was in Persia he was cast into the lion's den.

Now, no matter where his former colleagues in the school of the magi thought numbers came from,[42] Daniel believed God had created them and that He had revealed their secrets through agents like the 'palmoni'—an angelic visitor sometimes dubbed *the Wonderful Numberer*. It's my personal belief that, when Daniel was taken away to Persia, he left behind him a specific prophecy for the magi. The scroll of Daniel, written partly in Hebrew and partly in Aramaic, was for his own people. But for his Chaldean colleagues, I believe he produced a simple diagram, readily memorable, easily sketched and effortlessly transmissible intact century after century. Using the original sense of a degree as a measure of time,[43] a five-pointed star can be interpreted to find the location and year of the birth of the Messiah! I believe that half a millennium after Daniel left Babylon a group of magi followed the instructions encoded in the 'star' to find the one born 'king of the Jews.'[44]

---

42 The question of where numbers come from is still a debatable point today. Some people think mathematics is *discovered* and some people think it is *invented*. Those who think it's *invented* believe mathematics to be a creation of humanity; those who think it is *discovered* believe that it is already in existence on some plane, ready to be found. Those who think it is *discovered* need not necessarily believe it is created by God; some are neo-Platonists who believe in a dimension containing ideal forms.

43 Modern mathematics still retains that ancient connection of angles with time through the sub-division of a degree into sixty minutes and the further sub-division of a minute into sixty seconds.

44 See Anne Hamilton, *The Singing Silence: Jesus and the Healing of History #5*, Armour Books 2021 for details on how this could have been achieved.

2.5 The Golden Beginning

THERE'S NO QUESTION IN MY MIND that Daniel knew the profound importance of the golden ratio (which, to three significant figures, is 0.618 : 1). It is integral to the Word of God and is encoded no less than three times in the first seven words of Genesis alone. Transcribed into English these words, with vowels inserted, are: *bereshit bara Elohim et hashamayim ve'et ha'arets*. Now recall there were no separate digits in either Greek or Hebrew. The letters of the alphabet had numerical values. Here are the summations for each of the seven words:

$$
\begin{aligned}
\text{bereshit} &= 913 \\
\text{bara} &= 203 \\
\text{Elohim} &= 86 \\
\text{et} &= 401 \\
\text{hashamayim} &= 395 \\
\text{ve'et} &= 407 \\
\text{ha'arets} &= 296
\end{aligned}
$$

$$
\left.\begin{aligned}
\text{bara} + \text{ha'arets} &= 499 \\
\text{et} + \text{ve'et} &= 808
\end{aligned}\right\} \quad 499 \div 808 \approx 0.618
$$

$$
\left.\begin{aligned}
\text{bara} + \text{et} + \\
\text{ve'et} + \text{ha'arets} &= 1307
\end{aligned}\right\} \quad 808 \div 1307 \approx 0.618
$$

$$
\left.\begin{aligned}
\text{bara} + \text{Elohim} + \text{et} + \\
\text{ve'et} + \text{ha'arets} &= 1393 \\
\text{bereshit} + \text{bara} + \text{et} \\
+ \text{ve'et} + \text{ha'arets} &= 2220
\end{aligned}\right\} \quad 1393 \div 2220 \approx 0.62
$$

In addition to these close approximations to the golden ratio, there are several multiples of 111, the number of oneness associated with covenant:

$$\text{bereshit} + \text{Elohim} = 999$$
$$\text{bara} + \text{et} + \text{hashamayim} = 999$$
$$\text{Elohim} + \text{hashamayim} + \text{ve-et} = 888$$
$$\text{bereshit} + \text{bara} + \text{Elohim} + \text{et} + \text{hashamayim} = 1998$$
$$= 2 \times 999$$

Furthermore, as Ivan Panin demonstrated, many multiples of seven are encoded in this text. These include but are not limited to:

- the number of *Hebrew* words (7)
- the number of *Hebrew* letters[45] (28 = 4 × 7)
- the number of *Hebrew* letters in the first three words (14 = 2 × 7)
- the number of *Hebrew* letters in the last four words (14 = 2 × 7)
- the fourth and fifth words together have seven letters
- the sixth and seventh words together have seven letters
- *God*, *heaven* and *earth* together have fourteen letters
- the combined numerical value of the first and last letters of all the words is 1393 (7 × 199), which is the same as the combined value of the second, third, fourth, sixth and seventh words.

---

45 In the original Hebrew there were no vowels, so if you try to count up the letters in the English transliteration which have vowels inserted, it won't match the values here.

Now these sevens are interesting but what's mind-blowing is that seven—*exactly* seven!—can be created by using the golden ratio and the inverse square rule. Although you may never have heard of the inverse square rule before, it's the basic mathematical principle behind the operation of gravitational force. It describes the binding of the universe together. Since both the golden ratio and a sequence of sevens are so prominent in the statement of creation, it's possible that a simple pairing of the inverse square rule and the golden ratio is the master blueprint behind creation.

Now the relationship between the golden ratio and seven might not seem particularly mindboggling if you don't have enough mathematical background to appreciate that the golden ratio is an infinite decimal—it's non-repeating and also unending. Yet it becomes finite through a simple process of adding its square to its inverse square![46]

Now in case that last sentence seemed like esoteric gobbledegook—particularly if you have a mathematical phobia—let me translate it: *just as the numerically infinite can become numerically finite in mathematics, so the infinite Word became finite.* Infinity became limited. The unencompassed and unencompassable Word became

---

46 For you mathematical nerds, here it is in all its wondrous awesomeness so you can check it out for yourselves. Now because, I hope, only nerds will be reading this footnote, let me point out why I'm not using the more common term *phi*, Φ. Historically speaking, *phi* was introduced in the late nineteenth century. It is named for Phidias, a classical Greek sculptor, and was a successful attempt by humanists to replace the older term that was used by Leonardo da Vinci and many artists and mathematicians of his circle: *the Divine Proportion*. Phi is *not* the same as the golden ratio. Phi is a growth factor and can be approximated by 1.618, while its inverse, *little phi*, ϕ, can be approximated by 0.618, thus having the same digits as 0.618 : 1, the normal approximation for the golden ratio. Rather than use 0.618 in the following equations, the exact value ($0.5 \times \sqrt{5} - 0.5$) is used.

$(0.5 \times \sqrt{5} - 0.5)^2 + 1/(0.5 \times \sqrt{5} - 0.5)^2 = 3$ — *or* — $\phi^2 + 1/\phi^2 = 3$

$(0.5 \times \sqrt{5} - 0.5)^4 + 1/(0.5 \times \sqrt{5} - 0.5)^4 = 7$ — *or* — $\phi^4 + 1/\phi^4 = 7$

incarnate within the boundaries of flesh and was born as a child in Bethlehem.

He was full of grace and truth; the genuine ideal Man: Jesus of Nazareth.

'How big is God?' is a favourite question of children whose minds are trying to grapple with the vastness of the universe. Bigger, of course, than the entire cosmos and yet as small as a newborn baby.

2.6 Creation's Clothing

THE FIRST SENTENCE IN JOHN'S GOSPEL is composed of 17 words. Their numerical values are as follows:

(1)   En   = 55
(2)   arche = 719
(3)   en   = 58
(4)   ho   = 70
(5)   Logos = 373
(6)   kai   = 31
(7)   ho   = 70
(8)   Logos = 373
(9)   en   = 58
(10) pros = 450
(11) ton   = 420
(12) Theon = 134
(13) kai   = 31
(14) Theos = 284
(15) en   = 58
(16) ho   = 70
(17) Logos = 373

Embedded in this mathematical coding are allusions to the creation numerics of Genesis 1:1. Let's return our focus briefly to three significant words in the opening verse of Genesis.

God:	*elohim* =	86
The heavens:	*hashamayim* =	395
The earth:	*ha'arets* =	296

Add these together and we obtain 777. That's right—here are some more sevens in the creation sequence!

It doesn't take long to discover that John's echoes of the first line of Genesis extend beyond words into mathematics. The second and third word (and therefore, of course, the second and ninth word as well as the second and fifteen word) add up to 777. The fifth, sixth and eighth words add up to 777. So do the fifth, sixth and seventeenth, as well as the fifth, thirteenth and seventeenth, along with the sixth, eighth, and seventeenth, not to mention the eighth, thirteenth and seventeenth. That's seven lots of 777.

All very nifty. Undeniably cool.

But does it *mean* anything? Should we even expect it to be able to translate the symbolism of '777' other than to say it's a pointer to creation?

Whenever I've read books on numerical literary style, I find the authors have wrangled the numbers superbly, uncovered the hidden arithmetic or geometry, but then expected the results to proclaim their own design. However when design is divorced from meaning, its very intricacy makes it seem too arcane to be credible. Unfortunately, very few researchers venture to suggest a possible meaning.

I don't believe in mathematics for mathematics' sake. To apply postmodern deconstruction to ancient texts is, in my view, completely inappropriate. So, for me, the interpretation of symbolism of 777 rests on:

(1) discovering what 111 means, since 777 is 7 × 111
(2) looking for other appearances of 777 in Scripture, particularly in combination with the golden ratio

Now, obviously, 777 and the golden ratio appear in Genesis 1:1. But they also, perhaps, surprisingly appear in Paul's description of the Armour of God.

> *Therefore take up the full armour of God, so that when the day of evil comes, you will be able to stand your ground, and having done everything, to stand. Stand firm then, with the belt of truth buckled around your waist, with the breastplate of righteousness arrayed, and with your feet fitted with the readiness of the gospel of peace. In addition to all this, take up the shield of faith, with which you can extinguish all the flaming arrows of the evil one. And take the helmet of salvation and the sword of the Spirit, which is the word of God. Pray in the Spirit at all times, with every kind of prayer and petition. To this end, stay alert with all perseverance in your prayers for all the saints.*
>
> Ephesians 6:13–18[BSB]

In Greek, this passage is 101 words and its gematria—numerical value—is 77791. Adding 1 for the 'silence',[47] 77792 is divisible by

---

47 In gematria, a numerical value is assigned to each letter and these can be added to find the total for a word, a sentence, a passage or indeed a whole book of the Bible. The *kollel* or 'one more' may sometimes be added to the total. According to David Patterson, the addition of the *kollel* is not simply for the word itself but for the silence within the word. See: David Patterson, *Wrestling with the Angel: Towards a Jewish Understanding of the Nazi Assault on the Name*, Paragon House 2006.

17, by 52 and by 22. It has many other factors,[48] but these would have been the evocative ones for the original recipients of the letter. 77792 is also close enough to 77777 to call it immediately to mind.

Can we tell from Paul's clues what these numbers—111, 777 and 101—actually mean? I believe that, by drawing on the patterns of use in this sequence and elsewhere, we truly can. Without going into deep explanation, I'll simply say:

111 refers to covenant.

777 refers to covenantal defence.

101 refers to God's sustaining power.

This lets us know that all those multiples of 111 in Genesis 1:1 testify to God's covenantal nature. The 777 in both John and Genesis allude to God kissing His creation with protective armour. The number 101 in both places points beyond God's creative power to His sustaining and maintaining power.

In the very first line of his gospel, John used the very same numbers as Paul used for the design elements in the description of the Armour of God—17, 111, 777 and 101. John's message is not just about the Word as the Creator but as the One who clothed His creation in a shield of defence.[49]

---

48 Those factors are: 1, 2, 4, 8, 11, 13, 16, 17, 22, 26, 32, 34, 44, 52, 68, 88, 104, 136, 143, 176, 187, 208, 221, 272, 286, 352, 374, 416, 442, 544, 572, 748, 884, 1144, 1496, 1768, 2288, 2431, 2992, 3536, 4576, 4862, 5984, 7072, 9724, 19448, 38896, 77792.

49 This section is, of course, 777 words.

2.7 The Healing Tree

At the beginning of John's gospel, the flow of the story introduces the Word who was God and who was with God and who *'became flesh and made His dwelling among us.'*

The infinite pours Himself out and becomes finite. The eternal allows Himself to be bounded by space and time. And yet, by the end of the gospel, the flow reverses: the actions of Jesus as a finite human being cannot be described within the bounds of this world—the books about His poetic work would reach for infinity.

The world indeed cannot contain the words about the Word. As noted previously, Brian Simmons[50] rendered John's conclusion: *'The world itself would be emptied out into the books that would be*

---

50 Please note: I don't want to give the impression that I am endorsing *The Passion Translation* by quoting several times from it. I am doing so with care and caution where I find its insights deep, heart-stirring, soul-lifting and also (in my view, of course) accurate. Brian Simmons has done a wonderful thing in introducing people to a warm and tender intimacy with Jesus. However, his work is more a targum than a translation. It is full of interpretative glosses and clarifying opinions within the text itself, rather than restricting them to the margins. It is one thing to dig for the Aramaic thinking behind the text, it is another to impose a late fifth century translation back several centuries and reinterpret our earliest texts on that basis. As a *commentary*, his work would be wonderful; as a *translation*, it is misleading. See, for a very fine and balanced exposition of the problems: thinktheology.co.uk/blog/article/whats_wrong_with_the_passion_translation (accessed 29 November 2021)

written.' And John Gill's *Exposition of the Bible* refers to a similar rabbinic sentiment: 'If all the seas were ink, and the bulrushes pens, and the heavens and the earth volumes, and all the children of men were scribes, they would not be sufficient to write the law.'

It perhaps seems that John was indulging in excessive hyperbole when he intimated that the actions of Jesus as a finite human being are infinite in extent. Surely it would have been possible to write a timeline of events and speeches? It might have taken many dozens of volumes to accomplish the task, perhaps even hundreds, but that is not unlimited, unbounded, immeasurable.

Yet, I think John is right. The repercussions of what Jesus said and did spread out through time, branching endlessly into ever finer twigs—each of which carries a leaf for the healing of the nations. The impact of His actions cannot be delimited to the present. Nor does it simply go forward into the future; it also affects the past. The healings Jesus performed reached back into deep historical wounds, drawing out the septic poison of centuries. His encounter with the woman at the well in Samaria, for example, speaks into the pernicious rifts caused by the arrogance of David's grandson, along with the political decisions of the returned exiles. Simply by asking a foreign woman for a drink, He invites her to be His cupbearer and thereby mends the division caused by another cupbearer—Nehemiah—who had once enforced the exile of foreign women.

The actions of Jesus resound across millennia, healing today, saving today, transforming today.

When my sister was very young, she heard the story of the assassination of the Roman emperor Caligula. It distressed her greatly and she decided to pray for Caligula—and his horse, of course. The fact that Caligula had been dead for nearly two millennia wasn't relevant in her view. She reasoned that God is the Lord of time and that answering such a prayer is no harder to Him than making water run uphill.

The healings of Jesus are like water running uphill and downhill as well as pooling in the present. They work back and forward through time, healing hearts, homes and history.

Part

In the beginning was THE WORD, *and* THE WORD *was* WITH GOD, *and* THE WORD WAS GOD.

John 1:1 ESV

Three

He was **WITH GOD** in the beginning. **THROUGH HIM** all things were made, and **WITHOUT HIM** nothing was made that has been made.

In Him was **LIFE**, and that **LIFE** was the **LIGHT OF MEN**.

The **LIGHT** shines in the darkness, and the darkness has not overcome it.

John 1:2-5 BSB

3.1 An Abominable Beauty

In the beginning was the Word, and the Word was with God, and the Word was God.

John 1:1ESV

SEVENTEEN WORDS.

I imagine John, *son of thunder*, smiling ever so slightly as he finished this first line. It's not a nice smile. He might have mellowed over the years, exhorting his children in the faith to love, love and then love some more. But this verse about the LOGOS is a moment of fierce truth. 'Take that!' he's saying to the Gnostics. 'Seventeen words about the LOGOS.'[51]

When it came to heresy, John drew a line in the sand and taught those he mentored to do the same. Irenaeus, having told Polycarp's story of John dashing out of the bath-house on discovering Cerinthus was under the same roof, immediately followed it with a story about Polycarp himself.[52]

One particular heretic, Marcion, met Polycarp on one occasion and asked, 'Do you know me?'

Polycarp replied, 'I do know you, first-born of Satan.'

---

51 It's seventeen words both in English and in Greek.
52 earlychristianwritings.com/text/irenaeus-book3.html (accessed 11 July 2021)

Seventeen words about the Logos is an insult of that order to Gnostic sensibilities. It's an opening salvo in a theological conflict and, despite the fact the combination of seventeen with the Logos means nothing whatsoever to most modern believers, it would have been almost a seismic shock to John's original audience. Today's readers wouldn't even notice there *are* seventeen words, let alone consider the number significant. However there would have been nothing subtle about this word count in the past. John might as well have lobbed a grenade into the opening line. That's how explosive it is.

He'd started his gospel with one of the archetypes of mathematical beauty—the Logos—but then, by the end of the sentence, he'd thrown in a bombshell. Blending seventeen and the Logos is an iconoclastic mix that would have horrified the Greek literati of the time: no one with a taste for 'the good, the true and the beautiful' would have fused the two together.

Thomas Merton in *The Seven Storey Mountain* expressed a frustration that must be akin to the aggravation John experienced: 'I got to a state where phrases like "the Good, the True, and the Beautiful" filled me with a kind of suppressed indignation, because they stood for the big sin of Platonism: the reduction of all reality to the level of pure abstraction, as if concrete, individual substances had no essential reality of their own, but were only shadows of some remote, universal, ideal essence filed away in a big card-index somewhere in heaven, while the demi-urges milled around the Logos piping their excitement in high, fluted, English intellectual tones.'

The Logos of Platonism is not the Logos of Christianity. The first is a deified mathematical abstraction; the second incarnated flesh-and-blood. In the ancient world, the mathematical *Logos* was what we call the golden ratio today: for the Pythagoreans, it was a number-god, indicating to them that their founder had been re-incarnated as Jesus.

Now, according to Plutarch, seventeen was considered by the Pythagoreans to be an abomination.[53] Platonism and Pythagoreanism were the philosophies behind Greek literary design, and they went hand in hand in early Gnosticism. In fact, they even go hand in hand in twenty-first century Gnosticism, as evidenced by *The Da Vinci Code*, which mixes expansive details about the golden ratio with Gnostic traditions from the third century about Mary Magdalen.

John kills this notion immediately. He hardly even allows the idea a chance to form before he takes aim with a flaming dart. By mixing seventeen, the 'abominable' number, with the Logos he was, in the eyes of the literati, blending the repulsive and the gorgeous: they would have considered it grotesque.

But what did the Christians think of seventeen?

---

53 In Plutarch's *Morals*, he explains the significance of 17 while discussing the myth of Isis and Osiris: 'On the seventeenth day of the month took place, as the Egyptians fable, the death of Osiris, on which day the full Moon being completed becomes most conspicuous: on which account the Pythagoreans call that day "Antiphraxis" (*precaution*); and generally abominate that particular number, for sixteen being a square number and eighteen having sides of unequal length which alone of the integral numbers have the peculiarity of possessing external measurements equal to the areas contained by them, the seventeen intruding hedges off and disjoins them from one another, and distracts the proportion of one to eight, because it is itself cut up into unequal parts.' (sacred-texts.com/cla/plu/pte/pte04.htm accessed 10 July 2021)

3.2 A Splash of Seventeens

It's probably not the sort of check that's crossed your mind. However if you've ever spotted a long list in one of the gospels or epistles and bothered to count the number of items, you might have noticed the prevalence of seventeen. One such tally might be explained away as happening by random chance, but the recurrence indicates seventeen was a deliberate choice on the part of the author. Consider, for instance, the nature of love in 1 Corinthians 13:

(1) *patient*
(2) *kind*
(3) *not envious*
(4) *not boastful*
(5) *not proud*
(6) *not rude*
(7) *not self-seeking*
(8) *not easily angered*
(9) *forgiving of wrongs*
(10) *does not delight in evil*
(11) *rejoices with the truth*
(12) *always protects*
(13) *always trusts*
(14) *always hopes*
(15) *always perseveres*
(16) *never fails*
(17) *remains forever*

Or consider another aspect of love, as mentioned in Romans 8:35–39. *'Who shall separate us from the love of Christ?'* Paul asked. *'Shall*

(1) *trouble*
(2) *hardship*
(3) *persecution*
(4) *famine*
(5) *nakedness*
(6) *danger*
(7) *sword*

As it is written: 'For your sake we face death all day long; we are considered as sheep to be slaughtered.' No, in all these things we are more than conquerors through him who loved us. For I am convinced that neither

(8) *death*
(9) *life*
(10) *angels*
(11) *demons*
(12) *the present*
(13) *the future*
(14) *any powers*
(15) *height*
(16) *depth*
(17) *anything else in all creation*

will be able to separate us from the love of God that is in Christ Jesus our Lord.'

Check out any of the lists in the epistles and gospels and it soon becomes apparent that this number is by far the favourite, and is used at every possible opportunity. It isn't just Paul. Luke's account of the Day of Pentecost contains a list of the language groups who heard Peter speak:

Now there were staying in Jerusalem God-fearing Jews from every nation under heaven. When they heard this sound, a crowd came together in bewilderment, because each one heard them speaking in his own language. Utterly amazed, they asked: 'Are not all these men who are speaking Galileans? Then how is it that each of us hears them in his own native language?

(1) Parthians
(2) Medes
(3) Elamites
(4) residents of Mesopotamia
(5) Judea
(6) Cappadocia
(7) Pontus
(8) Asia
(9) Phrygia
(10) Pamphylia
(11) Egypt
(12) parts of Libya
(13) near Cyrene
(14) visitors from Rome (Jews)
(15) visitors from Rome (converts to Judaism)
(16) Cretans
(17) Arabs

we hear them declaring the wonders of God in our own tongues!' Amazed and perplexed, they asked one another, 'What does this mean?'

Acts 2:5–12[NIV]

In addition:

- there are 17 mentions of 'Father' in Matthew's version of the Sermon on the Mount as well as 17 references to Jesus as 'the Christ' throughout his gospel;
- Matthew also includes 17 prayers;
- there are 17 mentions of bread in the 'Bread Portion' of Mark's gospel;
- there's a requirement of 17 qualities for those who desire the 'noble task' of an elder;
- 17 uses of 'to know the truth' occur in the first epistle of John;
- there are 17 times that, in his gospel, John qualifies 'zoe', *life*, with the adjective *eternal*;
- 17 times he calls Peter 'Simon' and 17 times he uses 'semeion', *sign* or *miracle*.
- Paul makes 17 references to joy in Philippians;[54]
- he also uses 'sophia', *wisdom*, 17 times in his first letter to the Corinthians;
- he quotes the prophet Isaiah 17 times in his letter to the Romans;
- he cites 17 names in his personal remarks at the end of the second letter to Timothy;
- he mentions 17 'perils' that he's survived in 2 Corinthians 11:23–26.
- In the book of Revelation, the word 'nikao', *overcome*, is used 17 times and there are 17 promises made to the overcomer.

There are 17 faith heroes listed in the eleventh chapter of Hebrews,[55] and in the following chapter there's another list of 17, divided in the same 7:10 partition as the list of things that cannot separate from the love of God in Romans. This time the list is about approaching God:

---

54 16 of which are based on the Greek word 'chara' and one based on 'kauchaomai'.
55 The 'golden ratio' spot, position number 11, is marked by the only woman in the list—Rahab.

You have not come:

(1) *to a mountain that can be touched*
(2) *to burning fire*
(3) *to darkness*
(4) *to gloom*
(5) *to storm*
(6) *to a trumpet blast*
(7) *to a voice speaking such words that those who heard it begged that no further word be spoken to them, because they could not bear what was commanded.*

… But you have come:

(8) *to Mount Zion*
(9) *to the heavenly Jerusalem*
(10) *to the city of the living God*
(11) *to thousands upon thousands of angels*
(12) *to the joyful assembly*
(13) *to the church of the firstborn, whose names are written in heaven*
(14) *to God, the judge of all men*
(15) *to the spirits of righteous men made perfect*
(16) *to Jesus the mediator of a new covenant*
(17) *to the sprinkled blood that speaks a better word than the blood of Abel.*

See to it that you do not refuse Him who speaks. If they did not escape when they refused Him who warned them on earth, how much less will we, if we turn away from Him who warns us from heaven?

Hebrews 12:18–25

There are 17 appearances of angels in the gospels and the book of Acts:

(1) To *Joseph* in Matthew 1:20
(2) To *Joseph* in Matthew 2:13
(3) To *Joseph* in Matthew 2:19
(4) To *Jesus* in Matthew 4:11
(5) On the *stone* in Matthew 28:2
(6) Inside the *tomb* in Mark 16:5
(7) To *Zachary* in Luke 1:11
(8) To *Mary* in Luke 1:26
(9) To *shepherds* in Luke 2:9
(10) To *shepherds* in Luke 2:13
(11) To *Jesus* in Luke 22:43
(12) At the *Pool of Bethesda* in John 5:4
(13) To the *disciples* in Acts 1:11
(14) To the *disciples* in prison in Acts 5:19
(15) To *Cornelius* in Acts 10:3
(16) To *Peter* in prison in Acts 12:7
(17) To *Paul* in Acts 27:23

There are many other seventeens too.[56] But of course, if John's gospel truly is paired front-and-back, then another significant reference to seventeen should appear towards the end. This is found, explicitly and unmistakably, in John 21:11 which describes a haul of 153 fish. Now this is a mathematical joke and demonstrates how much fun Jesus was having after the resurrection. It's really exceptionally clever. However humour and poetry are the first casualties of translation and this particular joke requires a knowledge of ancient mathematical terms. 153 is 9 times 17, and is also the 17th 'triangular number'—a concept holding sacred overtones for the Greeks. Both the explanation of

---

56 There are 17 prophetic books in the Hebrew Scriptures as well as 17 historical books (and 5 poetical books). Psalm 83:6–12 mentions 17 enemies of the people of Israel, a tenfold contemporary confederation and seven enemies destroyed in the past. There are also 1717 references to 'land' across the Old and New Testaments.

the joke and the concept of triangular numbers are discussions I'll defer until later.

At this point, I'd prefer to look at the significance of 17 to the early disciples. What prompted Matthew, Mark, Luke, John and Paul to use it so often? Was it simply to counter the infiltration of the Pythagorean Gnostics? Was it about making an unequivocal statement that Jesus was not Pythagoras re-incarnated?

Frankly, I think a negative reason for using 17 is important, but not sufficient. There must be a positive reason as well. Seventeen may point to the date of the resurrection. Jesus rose from the dead on the 17th day of the month of Nisan.[57] This date corresponds to two historical events: it was the day Noah's ark came through the waters of the flood to rest on the top of Mount Ararat and it was the date the Israelites came through the waters of the Sea during the Exodus.

There's a sense then in which it symbolises the culmination of redemption and the reaching of a safe harbour on the far side of catastrophic disaster.[58]

However, *one* of my conclusions is that 17 is shorthand for 70. In both Hebrew and Greek there is considerable ambiguity regarding mathematical operations. It is uncertain, for example, whether Jesus responded to Simon's question about how many times he should forgive a repentant brother with 'seventy times seven' or 'seventy plus seven'. Is it 490 or is it 77?

---

[57] The word Nisan is said to derive from 'nitzan' meaning *bud*, or 'nissim' meaning *miracles* or *redemption*, and possibly being related to a Sumerian word for *firstfruits*.

[58] This might be foreshadowed in the Book of Jeremiah. Some commentaries say Jeremiah offered 17 prayers on behalf of the people of Judah, before stopping at God's command. After he stopped, he then bought a field at a cost of 17 shekels—showing his faith in the return of the exiles to Judah after the calamity of the Babylonian invasion and the enslavement of the people.

Because of the same ambiguity, it is difficult to differentiate between 7 + 10 and 7 x 10. Now, if 17 is indeed a pointer to 70, it is simple to understand. For the Hebrew people, 70 symbolised the nations of the world and their governments. Genesis 10 lists seventy descendants of Noah who gave their names to various lands, while Deuteronomy 32:8 affirms that God apportioned the inheritance for the nations according to the 70 descendants of Jacob, though some manuscripts say He divided it up according to the number of the 'angels of God'. Now of course, there are thousands upon thousands of angels, but when it refers to the angel-shepherds who rule the nations, this would again point to 70—to the principalities, the dark fallen powers, who ruled from the Mount of Assembly. These powers 'behind the throne' of various kings and emperors were the seventy 'young lions', the so-called sons of the goddess Asherah.

When Jesus sent out a band of seventy disciples in groups of two, He was deliberately creating a new kind of government—one that specialised in healing, restoration and repentance. Derek Prince in *Rediscovering God's Church* suggested the closest Hebrew equivalent to the Greek word Jesus used for His church—'ekklesia'—is 'knesset', the name for the current Israeli parliament.

It's my view then that *one* purpose of 17 is to indicate 70. It symbolises the church of Christ as a divine parliament, instituted by Him for the re-creation of the earth.

PART

In Him was life, and that life was the light of all mankind. The light shines in the darkness, and the darkness has not overcome it. There was a man sent from God whose name was John. He came as a witness to testify concerning that light, so that through him all might believe. He himself was not the light; he came only as a witness to the light. The true light that gives light to everyone was coming into the world.

JOHN 1:4-14 NV

He was in the world, and though the world was made through Him, the world did not recognise Him. He came to that which was His own, but His own did not receive Him. Yet to all who did receive Him, to those who believed in His name, He gave the right to become children of God—children born not of natural descent, nor of human decision or a husband's will, but born of God. The Word became flesh and made His dwelling among us.

FOUR

Peter turned around and saw the disciple whom Jesus loved following them — the one who also had leaned back on His chest at the supper and said, 'Lord, who is the one who is betraying You?' So Peter, upon seeing him, said to Jesus, 'Lord, and what about this man?'

JOHN 21:20-24 NASB

Jesus said to him, 'If I want him to remain until I come, what is that to you? You follow Me!' This saying therefore went out among the brethren that that disciple would not die; yet Jesus did not say to him that he would not die, but only, 'If I want him to remain until I come, what is that to you?' This is the disciple who bears witness of these things, and wrote these things; and we know that his witness is true.

4.1 The Light of the World

> *In Him was life, and that life was the light of all mankind. The light shines in the darkness, and the darkness has not overcome it. There was a man sent from God whose name was John. He came as a witness to testify concerning that light, so that through him all might believe. He himself was not the light; he came only as a witness to the light. The true light that gives light to everyone was coming into the world.*
>
> John 1:4–13[NIV]

Seven times John mentions that Jesus is the Light.[59] Once again he directs our attention back to the sevens of Genesis. He also reminds us of God's creative act when His word brings forth Light.

> *And God said, 'Let there be light'; and there was light.*
>
> Genesis 1:3[AMP]

Both the begetter of light and begotten as Light, Jesus embodies the mystery of the Creator becoming part of His creation. In the Hebrew of Genesis 1:3, God's declaration is simply an instruction for light to exist. He says: 'Be, light!'

Now my apologies once more. Please excuse this quick excursion,

---

[59] The last reference, strictly speaking, is *gives light* or *enlightens*, a verb rather than the noun for *light*. It is the Greek 'phōtízō' derived from 'phṓs', *light*.

not into mathematics on this occasion, but into English grammar. The verb 'to be' is parsed in the present tense as follows:

- I *am*
- you *are*
- he/she/it *is*
- we *are*
- they *are*

Because 'be' doesn't look like it's related to 'am', when it actually is, we miss the significance of the wording when God created light. The very first recorded Word uttered by God was 'be', the imperative of *His own name*.

This is the background to John's sevenfold use of 'light'. He's harking back to Creation again and telling us that the begetter of light and life and language has been begotten as the Light, the Life and the Word. Yet his vision encompasses both past and the future. He looks backwards to 'Be, light!' with its encoding of the 'I Am' of God's name, and he also looks ahead by foreshadowing the statement of Jesus, 'I Am the Light of the World'—one of the seven 'I Am' statements presented throughout the gospel.

However this reminder of light is *seven*fold, and is therefore suggestive of the menorah. The menorah was a seven-branched lampstand, of pure gold, with beaten metalwork cups in the shape of almond blossoms ringed with finely-wrought foliage. The golden cups formed seven oil lamps that suffused the sanctuary with light and fragrance. God gave Moses the instructions for the menorah, up to and including details for the wick trimmers. Finally He said:

> A talent of pure gold is to be used for the lampstand and all these accessories. See that you make them according to the pattern shown you on the mountain.
>
> Exodus 25:39–40[NIV]

The writer to the Hebrews reminds us that this admonition was to ensure that earthly things were based on divine blueprints and that the tabernacle showed forth the nature of heaven. All the items and objects that formed part of the sacrificial system in the tabernacle were designed to prefigure the ministry of Jesus.

> *They serve at a place that is a pattern, a shadow, of what is in heaven. When Moses was about to make the tent, God warned him, 'Be sure to make everything based on the plan I showed you on the mountain.'*
>
> Hebrews 8:5^{GWT}

John intentionally draws our minds back to the Tabernacle in the Wilderness—that partitioned tent where prayer and praise, worship and sacrifice was offered to God. We can be sure this was his purpose because he actually used the word 'tabernacle' to describe Jesus dwelling among us.

> *The Word became flesh and made His dwelling among us.*
>
> John 1:14^{BSB}

The Greek word for 'made His dwelling' is *to take up residence in a tent* or *to have a tabernacle*. It's not simply living in Nazareth or spending time in the towns of Galilee—this is about the presence of God in the midst of humanity. This is a sacred sanctuary, camping right in middle of society and hallowing it, consecrating it, making it holy.

Immanuel has come, long-promised, long-awaited but still unlooked for. '*He came to that which was His own, but His own did not receive Him.*'

4.2 The Coming of Immanuel

> *Now all this took place that what was spoken by the Lord through the prophet might be fulfilled, saying, 'Behold, the virgin shall be with child, and shall bear a Son, and they shall call His name Immanuel,' which translated means, God with us.*
>
> Matthew 1:22–23^{NASB}

MATTHEW'S GOSPEL REFLECTS ON THE words of Isaiah, indicating that the birth of Jesus was the fulfillment of prophecy. The king of Aram had allied himself with the king of Israel, and together they were intending to lay siege to Jerusalem. Isaiah had tried to bolster the courage of Ahaz, the king of Judah, in the face of this imminent attack. He told Ahaz to ask for a sign from heaven that the enemy alliance would collapse—to be as bold and extreme as he dared. But Ahaz said:

> *'I will not ask for a sign. I refuse to put the Lord to the test.'*
>
> Isaiah 7:12^{GNT}

> *Then Isaiah said: 'Hear now, you house of David! Is it not enough to try the patience of humans? Will you try the patience of my God also? Therefore the Lord Himself will give you a sign: The virgin will conceive and give birth to a son, and will call him Immanuel.'*
>
> Isaiah 7:13–14^{NIV}

Ahaz looks superficially pious and faithful as he refuses to test God. But in reality, he could hardly be more faithless. Jesus is well-known as the Second Adam. But was He also the *Second* Immanuel?

Some rabbis believe, on the basis of the record of the reign of Ahaz, that a child named Immanuel was indeed born in fulfillment of Isaiah's prophecy. So why is there no record of Immanuel's reign? After all, Isaiah's proclamation about him and the collapse of the invaders' plans—and indeed their own kingdoms—was very time-specific:

> *Before the boy knows how to refuse the evil and choose the good, the land whose two kings you dread will be deserted.*
>
> Isaiah 7:16[ESV]

At most, this refers to a few years, not to a long period of time. Isaiah is declaring a 'soon', not decades—or *centuries!*—of waiting. What could have happened that we know nothing of the contemporary fulfillment[60] of these words?

It is thought that Immanuel is the boy referred to in this verse about Ahaz:

> *He even sacrificed his own son as a burnt offering to idols, imitating the disgusting practice of the people whom the Lord had driven out of the land as the Israelites advanced.*
>
> 2 Kings 16:3[GNT]

---

60 The prophecy of Immanuel, particularly the section which declares the imminent collapse of the northern kingdom of Israel as well as the kingdom of Aram, is exceedingly problematic within our modern understanding of prophecy as *foretelling*. Isaiah was telling Ahaz there was nothing to fear, *so long as he trusted God*. So long as Ahaz had even the mustard-seed of faith to ask for a sign, God could show He was willing to make good on His word. However, Aram and Israel mounted a devastating attack on Jerusalem as described in 2 Kings 16:5–6. The placement of the comment about this invasion immediately after 2 Kings 16:3 suggests that the prophecy of Isaiah was not unconditional and that child sacrifice practiced by Ahaz was the reason it was not fulfilled.

That puts a wholly darker complexion on John's words: *'He came to that which was His own, but His own did not receive Him.'* But was John intending to evoke Immanuel? Matthew had been explicit, John seems a little too subtle. Was the comment, *'The Word became flesh and made His dwelling among us,'* an intentional pointer to Immanuel?

I think it was. And the reason I think so is that no other number says 'Immanuel' quite like 496.

4.3 Proclaiming Perfection

John's gospel, as we've seen, starts with 17 words. However, in poetry, the number of syllables is far more important than the number of words. In Greek, the opening Hymn to the Logos and prologue has 496 syllables.[61] The very last segment of the gospel in chapter 21 has 496 words. Even diehard skeptics who are doubtful about the whole concept of numerical literary style generally do not consider this to be coincidental.

So what is the significance of 496?

Mathematically it's intriguing, even today. Back in classical times, it was considered a 'perfect' number. That's one advantage in John's use of it: he was testifying that Jesus is, in every way, perfect.

---

61 Verses 1 to 18, as expounded by Richard Bauckham in *The Testimony of the Beloved Disciple: Narrative, History, and Theology in the Gospel of John*, Baker Academic 2007. In addition to the 496 of the prologue and finale, Bauckham also points out the section from John 1:19 to John 2:11 consists of 1550 syllables, which is the value of the phrase *ho Christos*, ('The Christ'). Moreover, the 'high priestly prayer' of Jesus to the Father in John 17:1b–26 consists of 486 words, and 486 is the numerical value of pater ('father'). He finally notes that the numerical value of 'Jesus' in Hebrew is the same as the numerical value of 'Lamb of God' in Hebrew, 391. So when John the Baptiser proclaims, 'Behold, the Lamb of God!' in John 1:29 and John 1:35–36, he is playing with the gematria (numerical value of the letters) of Jesus' name. See: www.psephizo.com/biblical-studies/secret-codes-in-the-bibleand-n-t-wright/ (accessed 10 June 2021)

Another is that the way he features 'chiasmus'—the back-and-front mirror scenes inspired by the structure of Hebrew poetry—would immediately remind educated Jews of the prophetic poetry of Isaiah. Poems written in the chiastic style have verses that are reflected around the centre like rings.

Andrew Bartelt[62] points out the 'ring' surrounding the prophecy of Immanuel is 496 syllables.

Now, you might think to yourself: who on earth would have known this back in the day? The answer is: the scribes—the *sopherim* whose job it was to copy scrolls, and to cross-check them by counting each letter, line, syllable, jot and tittle to ensure the text was duplicated exactly. 496 was exactly the kind of special number used to ensure that not even the smallest stroke of the pen had been missed or an element dropped out of the Law.

To these specialists, 496 shouted, 'This is the fulfillment of Isaiah's words about Immanuel, *God with us*.' Of course, to a Greek audience, it didn't have those connotations at all. Here again, John comes up with a solution with as much pure and simple genius as his choice of the word Logos. 496 might evoke different responses in different cultures but it didn't matter either way: it worked. And it worked brilliantly.

From ancient times, 496 was a so-called 'perfect' number. We still use that designation for it today. In fact, 496 is the third perfect number.

These numbers are classified as those which have factors that add up to the numbers themselves. The first perfect number is 6 because its factors (excluding 6 itself) are 1, 2 and 3 and these, when added together, equal 6. The second perfect number is 28 because its factors (excluding 28 itself) are 1, 2, 4, 7 and 14 and

---

62 Andrew H. Bartelt, *The Book around Immanuel: Style and Structure in Isaiah 2–12*, Eisenbrauns 1996.

these, when added together, equal 28. The third perfect number is 496 because its factors (excluding 496 itself) are 1, 2, 4, 8, 16, 31, 62, 124 and 248 and these, when added together, equal 496.

In other words, the Greeks to whom John was writing would have seen his gospel as starting and ending with 'perfection'. The Hymn to the Logos declares a beautiful and poetic message across the centuries but, in its original language, it also embedded the concept of mathematical perfection.

4.4 Children of God

But to all who did receive Him, who believed in His name, He gave the right to become children of God.

John 1:12^{ESV}

It was full of large fish, 153, but even with so many, the net was not torn.

John 21:11^{BSB}

AHH, DEEP SIGH. I'M NOT a big fan of gematria, the practice of calculating the value of a word and then matching it with another word of equal value. It's uncomfortable territory to say the least. But despite my preferences to the contrary, I realise that it's an undeniable current within the underground river of mathematical features flowing through the gospel.

Using Hebrew gematria, Richard Bauckham connects 153, mentioned as the number of fish caught by the disciples, with the 'children of God'.[63] This chiastic reflection is very subtle, particularly since it would be far more accurate to say '*sons of God*'—a reference to angelic hosts—has a numeric value of 153 in Hebrew, not '*children of God*.'

---

63 *The Testimony of the Beloved Disciple: Narrative, History, and Theology in the Gospel of John*, Baker Academic 2007, p281. D. R. Ahrendts (1898), Heinz Kruse S.J. (1960) and Joseph A. Romeo (1978) seem to have discovered this mathematical identity independently. (See Joseph A. Romeo, *Gematria and John 21:11—The Children of God*, Journal of Biblical Literature, 1978)

Nevertheless, what does 153 tell us about the 'children of God'? How does it clarify what it means to 'believe in His name'?

> *If you confess with your mouth, 'Jesus is Lord,' and believe in your heart that God raised Him from the dead, you will be saved.*
>
> Romans 10:9^{BSB}

So said Paul, emphasising that this belief is about the resurrection. And that's precisely what 153 does.

One of the remarkable features of 496—and it has many!—is that it is equal to the sum of the cubes of the first four odd numbers:

$$1^3 + 3^3 + 5^3 + 7^3 = 496$$

The sum of the cubes of the first three odd numbers is:

$$1^3 + 3^3 + 5^3 = 153$$

Now let me rearrange those numbers slightly: $1^3 + 5^3 + 3^3$.

Here is the skeleton of 153, 1 – 5 – 3, under a 'trinity'[64] function:

$$1^3 = 1$$
$$5^3 = 125$$
$$3^3 = \underline{27}$$

Add these up and the answer is 153—making it the *first* number that can be immediately 'resurrected' from its own skeleton by a trinity function.

We should be reminded of God's instruction to Ezekiel:

> *Prophesy to these bones, and say to them, 'O dry bones, hear the word of the Lord! Thus says the Lord God to these bones: 'Surely I will cause breath to enter into you, and you shall live.'*
>
> Ezekiel 37:4–5^{NKJV}

---

64 A trinity function is also called a cubic function.

Here, unearthed from the mathematics, is a claim of prophecy fulfilled. The 'bones' of the number 153 have become re-embodied back to their original form.

But that's not all! Just wait! There's an even more lovely relationship between 496 and 153. Instead of applying a trinity function, let's see what happens when 496 is multiplied by the *logos*.

$$496 \times 0.618 \approx 306$$

$$306 \div 2 = 153$$

Here we have an emblem of perfection (496), linked through the power of the Word who is life and light (*logos*, 0.618), to resurrection (153).

Ahh, deep sigh. Isn't that just so wondrously spectacular?[65]

---

[65] It should go without saying, but I will point it out anyway: these last three sections, and the next three as well, are each 496 words long. So too are all of the sections in Part 5, except the last one which is 1111 words long. If you are curious about the fourth perfect number, it's 8128. The fifth is 33,550,336 and the sixth 8,589,869,056. The seventh is 137,438,691,328.

4.5 Hidden Elegance

Beauty and mathematics—for us today it's such an unusual combination it's almost unthinkable. Back in the ancient world, however, poets and artists, sculptors and architects would never consider beginning their work without taking the canons of beautiful design into consideration. Even within mathematics itself, professionals have an appreciation for beautiful, elegant equations. When it comes to to identifying what is, in their opinion, the most supremely lovely of all, many mathematicians choose a particular formulation called Euler's Identity.[66] The first time I saw and understood it, I breathed 'Ahh!' in complete awe. One of my fellow students, an atheist, commented, 'It almost makes me believe God exists.'

Euler's Identity is stunning: it combines zero and one together with two common irrational numbers (that is, numbers that are non-repeating and keep going on to infinity as far as decimal places are concerned) and wraps them up with an imaginary number (that is, the square root of a negative number.) 0, 1, e, i, and π.

Here it is: $e^{i\pi} + 1 = 0$

---

[66] Named for Leonhard Euler, a Swiss mathematician, physicist, astronomer and engineer of the 18th century.

Now this may be more baffling than inspiring to you but don't let that put you off. Because Scripture makes reference to this equation! One of the irrational numbers here appears hidden in the background of Genesis 1:1 while the other occurs in John 1:1. It's difficult enough to come to grips with the presence of π, but how *e* could appear, apart from supernatural encoding, is impossible to explain. That's because the actual concept of *e*, the base of the natural logarithm,[67] was not discovered until the seventeenth century. As we've subsequently discovered, *e* is found throughout the natural world, particularly in systems where growth and decay are taking place.[68]

Circles are the way we usually encounter π. The relationship between a circle's radius and its circumference is 2πr. It was Archimedes, the most famous inventor of the ancient world who first approximated π as $^{22}/_{7}$, a fractional expression used because the Greeks didn't have today's decimal system. Now, of course, we abbreviate it to 3.14 or 3.141592654… These are sufficient for most practical purposes, even though computers have calculated to over a trillion decimal places. The records are sure never to end because π itself is unending.[69]

---

67 *e*, also known as Euler's number, is approximately 2.71828 and can be found many different ways. The simplest is the sum to infinity of $1 + 1/1 + 1/{1 \times 2} + 1/{1 \times 2 \times 3} + 1/{1 \times 2 \times 3 \times 4} + 1/{1 \times 2 \times 3 \times 4 \times 5} + \ldots \ldots \ldots$

68 One example in the Bible involves human lifetime after the Flood. If you plot the date vs age of the descendants of Shem when they died on a natural-log graph, you'll notice the shortening of lifetime is not random. See Genesis 11:10–20.

69 1 Kings 7:23 is often cited as one of the errors in the Bible, because it appears to give a value of 3 for π. This is a misunderstanding in how to read the embedded mathematics. A corrected calculation using the encoded approximation for π shows that the 14-metre circumference of the molten sea is specified to an accuracy better than 0.0004 of a metre. This is an error of 0.04%, an incredible achievement in the pre-computer pre-lasercutter age. See: Chuck Missler, khouse.org/articles/1998/158/ (accessed 26 February 2023)

As mentioned previously, Hebrew letters did double duty as numbers. So did Greek letters.[70] They were each assigned a value. And if we consider Genesis 1:1 and calculate

$$\frac{\text{the number of letters} \times \text{the product of the letters}}{\text{the number of words} \times \text{the product of the words}}$$

we get 3.1416×10^{17}. Ignoring the power of 10, we have π to four decimal places. This is an accuracy more than we normally require in the modern world.

Now consider the Greek wording of John 1:1 and perform exactly the same operation.

$$\frac{\text{the number of letters} \times \text{the product of the letters}}{\text{the number of words} \times \text{the product of the words}}$$

This time we get 2.7183×10^{40}, and once again ignoring the power of 10, we have displayed the value of *e*, a number that was not discovered until the seventeenth century.

Now, to be honest, I hate to leave it like this. One of the difficulties I have with numerical literary analysis is that the scholars who undertake the work of uncovering the ancient secrets of the scribes—the *sopherim* who should more accurately be called *counters*—hardly ever attempt to explain the symbolic meaning of what they've found. They expect the mathematics to speak for itself. I don't believe it does—at least not in the present age. That's why I have a go at interpreting the numbers of Scripture. I may not be right in my translations but I've presented the best possibility I can.

However, when it comes to π and *e*, I'm dumbstruck. The mystery is so weighty all I can do is think: 'Wow! How awesome

---

70 To see the value of the letter and words, consult the charts here: khouse.org/articles/2003/482/ (accessed 26 February 2023)

is that!' And I find it impossible to explain. The numbers are called 'transcendent' in mathematics but they also partake of the transcendent in a spiritual sense. And because I've never lost the ineffable sense of awe that Euler's Identity first evoked in me, that's the best I can do by way of explanation.

4.6 Children of Light

According to early testimony about the fourth gospel, John's motivation in writing it was to counter Gnostic heresy. Curiously, the teachings of Cerinthus were classified together with those of Simon Magus, the Samaritan convert who was so astounded by the miracles accompanying Philip's ministry. The story of Simon Magus immediately follows that of the death of the first martyr Stephen—and there might be more significance to this sequence than at first appears. It's thought Stephen's background was probably Samaritan, since his impassioned speech to the Sanhedrin seems to quote from the Samaritan version of the Pentateuch. Simon, like Cerinthus, became famous for his Gnostic teaching.

> *Now for some time a man named Simon had practiced sorcery in the city and amazed all the people of Samaria… And all the people, both high and low, gave him their attention and exclaimed, 'This man is rightly called the Great Power of God.' They followed him because he had amazed them for a long time with his sorcery. But when they believed Philip as he proclaimed the good news of the kingdom of God and the name of Jesus Christ, they were baptised, both men and women. Simon himself believed and was baptised. And he followed Philip everywhere, astonished by the great signs and miracles he saw.*

> When the apostles in Jerusalem heard that Samaria had accepted the word of God, they sent Peter and John to Samaria. When they arrived, they prayed for the new believers there that they might receive the Holy Spirit... Then Peter and John placed their hands on them, and they received the Holy Spirit.
>
> When Simon saw that the Spirit was given at the laying on of the apostles' hands, he offered them money...
>
> Peter answered: 'May your money perish with you, because you thought you could buy the gift of God!... You have no part or share in this ministry, because your heart is not right before God. Repent of this wickedness and pray to the Lord in the hope that He may forgive you for having such a thought in your heart. For I see that you are full of bitterness and captive to sin.'
>
> Then Simon answered, 'Pray to the Lord for me so that nothing you have said may happen to me.'
>
> After they had further proclaimed the word of the Lord and testified about Jesus, Peter and John returned to Jerusalem, preaching the gospel in many Samaritan villages.
>
> Acts 8:9–25^{NIV}

Acts 8:9–25 NIV

According to the Letter of the Apostles, written in the second century, Simon formed a sect called 'Children of Light'. It appears that his followers, by the end of the first century, mistakenly felt John's gospel supported their views: possibly because, after all, John seven times mentions the light as a prelude to his comments about the children of God. And possibly too, because it's clear that by including the story of the Samaritan woman John had an obvious desire to build bridges with Samaritan believers.[71]

---

[71] Edwin D Freed, *Did John Write His Gospel Partly to Win Samaritan Converts?*, Novum Testamentum, Vol. 12, Fasc. 3 (Jul., 1970), pp. 241-256, Brill

4.7 Big Fish and Little fish

*Early the next morning Jesus stood on the shore, but the disciples did not realise who He was. Jesus shouted, 'Friends, have you caught **anything**?'*

'No!' they answered.

So He told them, 'Let your net down on the right side of your boat, and you will catch some...'[72]

*They did, and the net was so full of **FISH** that they could not drag it up into the boat.*

*... Simon... jumped into the water... the other disciples stayed in the boat and dragged in the net full of **FISH**.*

*When the disciples got out of the boat, they saw some bread and a charcoal fire with **fish** on it. Jesus told His disciples, 'Bring some of the **fish** you just caught.' Simon Peter got back into the boat and dragged the net to shore. In it were 153 large **FISH**, but still the net did not rip.*

*Jesus said, 'Come and eat!' But none of the disciples dared ask who He was. They knew He was the Lord. Jesus took the bread in His hands and gave some of it to His disciples. He did the same with the **fish**.*

John 21:4–13^{CEV}

---

[72] Many translations say 'some fish' here in verse 6, but the original Greek does not include the word *fish*.

THERE'S A LOT OF HIDDEN SEVENS in this scene. For a start, seven of the disciples had returned to Galilee. Once there, Simon announced he intended to go fishing. He wasn't suggesting a casual evening's outing, but a clear-cut and unequivocal return to his former way of life.

Now the ease with which the disciples resume their previous occupation as fishermen suggests that, most likely, they were back at Simon's hometown of Bethsaida. If they weren't, then they had to have hired, borrowed or stolen a boat—and none of those options seem as likely as Simon simply picking up where he left off before meeting Jesus, and taking his old trawler out from Bethsaida onto the Sea of Galilee.

Now Bethsaida was the scene of several miracles. In fact, Jesus had once sent the disciples ahead of Him to Bethsaida after taking five barley loaves and two fish, giving thanks for them, and then multiplying them so extravagantly that twelve basketfuls were left over. So when the disciples come to the beach where Jesus has prepared a breakfast of bread and fish, surely all the events of that amazing day would have tumbled back into their memories.

Bread and fish outside Bethsaida: it's such evocative symbolism. Could the disciples really have missed the reminder of the moment when Andrew introduced a boy with a lunch of five loaves and two small fish to Jesus? I don't think so.

A quick count of the number of times fish are mentioned in the scene of the lakeside breakfast gives us a tally of seven.[73] Just as light is mentioned seven times at the opening of his gospel, so here John draws up a parallel with fish. These references are, however, a little more subtle than the ones to light. Three different words are used to designate fish.

---

73   Various English translations have more or less than seven. This count from the Greek does not include 'fishing', the verb form. It only tallies up nouns that describe actual types of fish or fish products.

First, there is 'prosphagion', which is only ever mentioned in Scripture this once, in John 21:5, and is here translated **anything**.[74] It's not that indefinite: 'prosphagion' is a fish paste or relish to go with bread.

Second, there is 'ichthyon', the big **FISH** that were found in the net.

And third, there is 'opsarion', the little ***fish*** that Jesus was cooking on His campfire.

According to John it was 'opsarion', *little fish*, that the boy gave to Jesus on the day when the loaves and fishes were multiplied.[75] And if the disciples were alert enough, they would have realised that the two little fish the boy had presented to Jesus had increased to 154 fish—153 from the boat and 1 on the campfire. This time the multiplication factor was 77.

Wordlessly, without a single spoken reprimand, Jesus communicated a message to His disciples: 'You are all forgiven. Receive My pardon for abandoning your calling.' For they would have known exactly what 77 meant to Jesus.[76]

> *Peter came to Jesus and asked, 'Lord, how many times shall I forgive my brother or sister who sins against me? Up to seven times?'*
>
> *Jesus answered, 'I tell you, not seven times, but seventy-seven times.'*
>
> Matthew 18:21–22[NIV]

---

74 Some versions translate it *fish*, and some render it as *meat*.

75 John 6:9. However John's 'opsarion' is a departure from Matthew 14:17, which says 'ichthus', as do both Mark 6:41 and Luke 9:16.

76 See Section 3.2 regarding the ambiguity in both Greek and Hebrew with respect to mathematical operations. 70 + 7 could also have been 70 x 7, so some translations render this answer of Jesus as seventy times seven, not seventy-seven.

The blessing and forgiveness of Jesus for Peter—but not just for Peter—are evident throughout this scene. He had warned them:

> *No man, having put his hand to the plough, and looking back, is fit for the kingdom of God.*
>
> Luke 9:62^{KJV}

Peter might have been the instigator, but there were no protests from the others about throwing away their calling. They all agreed. But here Jesus is, pardoning and restoring them, forgiving and re-commissioning, absolving and reinstating.

He's re-igniting their vocation. Perhaps that's why *seven fish* parallel *seven lights*. It certainly reads like a riddle: *why is a fish like a light?* The small hand-held clay lamps of the first century certainly have a fish-like appearance, but I doubt that's the answer. Just as Jesus is the Light of the World who calls us the 'light of the world', He is the Fish who leads out His little fishes.

The second century Christian apologist Tertullian wrote, 'We, little fishes, after the image of our ichthus,[77] Jesus Christ, are born in the water[78] nor are we safe but by remaining in it.'[79]

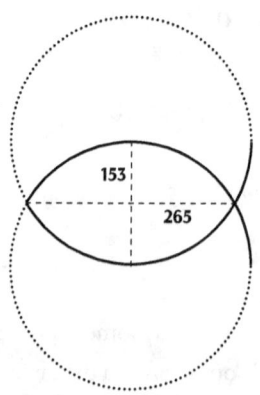

---

77 Greek word for *fish*. Also spelled 'ichthys' and 'ixthus'.
78 Baptism.
79 'De Baptismo', *On Baptism*.

4.8 Two Witnesses

As John's narrative progresses, matching names crop up continually. For example, Nathanael of Cana occurs at the beginning and then again at the end—the only two times he is ever mentioned in all of Scripture.

Mary, the mother of Jesus, parallels Mary Magdalene at the end. Both have a speaking role—the first at a wedding in Cana and the last in the garden outside the tomb. Both conversations revolve around bridal topics, the Magdalene's reflecting the betrothal scene in the *Song of Songs*. (Her title 'the Magdalene', by the way, has a numerical value of 153 in Greek.)

Nicodemus makes a significant appearance at the start. His reappearance at the end may seen almost inconsequential, but it provides a profound clue towards unravelling the mystery of the 'new birth' mentioned on the first occasion we hear of him.

Five disciples follow Jesus to Galilee at the start of the story; five 'groups' of disciples follow Him again to Galilee at the end. Both lists include Simon Peter and Nathanael. Those at the start are:

- Simon Peter
- Nathanael
- Andrew
- Philip
- an unnamed disciple

Those at the end are:

- Simon Peter
- Nathanael
- Thomas called Didymus
- sons of Zebedee
- two other unnamed disciples

The paralleling of names, particularly the Marys, Nathanael and Nicodemus, hints that the identity of the author was John. By positioning a mention of *'the man sent from God whose name was John'* in the same location at the front as the mention of the anonymous *'disciple who bears witness of these things'* at the back, the author seems to point to his own name.

Some commentators—Richard Bauckham for instance, once again—suggest this was not John the apostle, but John the elder. Regardless of that possibility, we do know that John the apostle was present in the final scene because he was one of the sons of Zebedee.

Both of these men named John were designated witnesses. The Baptiser came as *'a witness to the light'*, while the disciple maintains of himself that *'his witness is true.'* Both of them carry aspects of the spirit of Elijah—in fact, the comment that the rumour circulated that this *'disciple would not die'* appears to have been made in order to deliberately evoke Elijah. Apparently many early believers thought John the disciple would join the ranks of Enoch and Elijah, the only men in Scripture who had not died. A long-revered tradition spoke of Elijah as one of two witnesses—Moses being the other—who would return to identify the Messiah.[80]

This is an important clue to the interpretation of the last scene in the gospel: like the first scene it is evocative of Elijah the prophet. More than that, it identifies those who, in later ages, were given Elijah's mantle to carry on his legacy. But it is not John who received that appointment—as he himself testifies, he was there by the lakeside in Galilee when it was handed over to Peter.

---

80   Succoth 5a in the Talmud; Deuteronomy Midrash Rabbah 3. 239b

4.9 Moses and Elijah

> *'The facts of the case must be established by the testimony of two or three witnesses.'*
>
> Deuteronomy 19:15[NLT]

JOHN MAKES IT CLEAR RIGHT from the start that he is not the only witness. In so doing, he follows the precepts established by Moses: that the truth of a matter must be arrived at by two or more independent eyewitness accounts.

Now these witnesses do not necessarily have to be human. As we have seen, alef-tav, the fourth word of Genesis, is considered a faithful witness to creation because it is composed of *two* letters—and these particular living beings are the first and the last components of the Hebrew alphabet.

Just as our modern tendency is to regard letters as abstract, not living, so we think of heaven and earth as inanimate—but God does not. In Deuteronomy 4:26[NIV], He says, *'I call the heavens and the earth as witnesses against you this day.'* Heaven and earth are invoked as witnesses again in Deuteronomy 30:29 and 31:28 and 32:1 as well as Psalm 50:4 and Isaiah 1:2.

Joshua, as he reaffirmed the covenant at Shechem, said to the people:

> *'This stone will be a witness against us. It has heard all the words the Lord has said to us. It will be a witness against you if you are untrue to your God.'*
>
> Joshua 24:27^{NIV}

John, in his gospel, was not merely invoking his namesake and himself as witnesses but also the words of the gospel itself. We are pointed back to the opening of Genesis and the creation of the cosmos through the words of the Word: *In the beginning God created the heavens and the earth.*

As alef-tav were the first witnesses to the Logos, so the heavens and the earth have in turn become witnesses to the Logos, so John and John have, each in their respective times, witnessed to the Logos. But just as the bystanders at the scene of an accident will give varying accounts of events, so the witnesses to the Logos saw Him from different perspectives. It would be worrying if they didn't. We'd be dealing with an artfully constructed machination, rather than eyewitness statements.

John the apostle tells us the story of who Jesus is. The synoptic gospels tell us the story of what happened in the course of Jesus' life.

John begins with a fivefold identification of Jesus as:

- The Word
- The Creator
- The Lord
- The Life
- The Light

After identifying John the Baptiser as His witness, the apostle continues with his identification of Jesus:

- The Adopter
- The Visitor from heaven

As the One who gives the right to become children of God, He is the Adoptive Parent. Under Roman law, the one who decided an adoption could take place was the 'paterfamilias', *the male head of the family*. For early readers of the gospel, this verse about conferring the right to adoption would suggest that Jesus was the Head to whom the entire family was subject—just as was the case in the great patrician families of Rome. The title to all property and every aspect of inheritance was vested in the paterfamilias. Even adult sons could not make legally binding decisions without being granted his authority to do so.

Paul called Jesus the Head of the Body—here John evokes the same concept, but using cosmic imagery. Just as a Roman household with its slaves and servants, sons and daughters, was subject to the paterfamilias, so the Household of Heaven with its angels and prophets, along with children 'born of God', is subject to its Head, Jesus. We also have a foreshadowing here of the 'new birth' Jesus will later explain to Nicodemus.

When it comes to Jesus as the 'Visitor from heaven', we return to those faint and subtle hints about Elijah. Jesus is the Guest who comes to visit His own kinsmen but is rejected by them. He is unrecognised by the majority. Elijah likewise is a guest in Jewish tradition. An empty chair is put out as an invitation to him each Passover. He is also the one welcomed at the end of every Sabbath with the singing of hymns and summoned by name with a threefold formula of Elijah the prophet, Elijah the Tishbite and Elijah the Gileadite.

As mentioned, a strong expectation amongst the people of Judea and Galilee in the first century was that, when the Messiah came, Moses and Elijah would return to identify Him. Of course everyone thought their testimony would occur in public. While Jesus did in fact fulfill this popular tradition on the Mount of Transfiguration, the event was kept totally secret until after the resurrection.

We have seen His glory, the glory of the one and only Son from the Father, full of grace and truth.

PART

John 1:14 BSB

John 21:19 BSB

FIVE

Jesus said this to indicate the kind of death by which Peter would glorify God. And after He had said this, He told him, 'Follow Me.'

5.1 We Have Seen His Glory

> *We were eyewitnesses of His majesty. He received honour and glory from God the Father, and the voice was borne to Him by the Majestic Glory, 'This is My beloved Son, with whom I am well pleased.'*
>
> 2 Peter 1:17^{ESV}

JOHN WAS WITH HIS BROTHER JAMES and their friend, Simon the fisherman, who had—less than a week previously—just been renamed Cephas, when Jesus was transfigured before them. His clothes shone with a nonpareil whiteness as a cloud of numinous, spine-tingling glory descended and a Voice was heard, straight from the courts of heaven.

The three disciples were with Jesus, Moses and Elijah on the Mount of Transfiguration. It was the Feast of Tabernacles.

Luke's gospel opens with the story of the conception and birth of John the Baptiser, the Elijah-who-is-to-come, and also with the details of the conception and birth of John's cousin, Jesus of Nazareth. John's gospel seems to ignore such ordinary events in favour of cosmic wonder. Yet he does not entirely dismiss the conception narratives. Here, in this tiny flicker of a reference— *we have seen His glory, the glory of the one and only Son from the Father*—he harks back to the conception of the church. And, as he again says, it was an event he personally witnessed.

Just as Mary was overshadowed by the Holy Spirit, so Peter, James and John were overshadowed by the Father. They were impregnated with His words and the Word. Dwight Pryor reveals that God's statement is resonant with the language of a midwife.[81] This is a birth process where the notion of the divine Husband is fraught with complex and uncomfortable ideas for many moderns.

CS Lewis is often quoted as saying, 'God is so masculine, that He makes all of creation seem feminine in comparison.' More accurately, he wrote: 'The masculine none of us can escape. What is above and beyond all things is so masculine that we are all feminine in relation to it.'[82] Every Christian, regardless of gender, is part of the Bride of Christ.

Peter, James and John represented the disciples on the Mountain of Transfiguration. Out of this specific trio, the church would be born nearly nine months later.[83] At Pentecost, Peter was filled with

---

[81] See Dwight Pryor, *Jesus—The Fullness of Tanakh*, in John Fieldsend (ed.), Clifford Hill (ed.), Walter Riggans (ed.), John C.P. Smith (ed.), Fred Wright (ed.), *Roots and Branches: Explorations in the Jewish Context of the Christian Faith*, PVM Trust 1998

[82] CS Lewis, *That Hideous Strength*, Bodley Head 1945. In this finale to the science fiction trilogy, the hero Elwin Ransom addresses Jane Studdock: 'The male you could have escaped, for it exists only on the biological level. The masculine none of us can escape. What is above and beyond all things is so masculine that we are all feminine in relation to it.'

[83] The time between the Feast of Tabernacles (Booths or *Sukkot*) and the Feast of Weeks (Pentecost or *Shavuot*) varies from year to year. However, generally speaking, there is eight to eight-and-a-half months between them. Strictly speaking, I do not think that the events of the Transfiguration constitute the moment of conception of the church. I believe that the moment when that occurred was six days prior when, on the Day of Atonement (*Yom Kippur*), Jesus said to Simon, '*You are Peter and on this rock I will build My church.*' However I do believe the Transfiguration is the moment of 'implantation' of the church. In the natural, there is conception, implantation, pregnancy, birth. If implantation of the fertilised egg into the womb does not occur within six to eight days, then it will naturally abort. The Transfiguration, therefore, to my mind parallels this implantation.

the Spirit and, standing up with the Eleven, he delivered such a powerful call for repentance three thousand people were baptised and enrolled as Christian believers that very day.

The disciples, Simon in particular, had been impregnated by words of Jesus—*on this rock I will build My church*. That 'church', conceived and spoken into being on the Day of Atonement, was implanted by the Father six days later during the Feast of Tabernacles. The 'church' was then nurtured through a perilous pregnancy by the divine Midwife who brought it to birth on the day of Pentecost.

The glory that John testifies he has seen is not relegated to a single past event. It is present in the church all around him.

5.2 The Only

> And the Word became flesh and dwelt among us, and we have seen His glory, glory as of the only Son from the Father, full of grace and truth.
>
> John 1:14^{ESV}

'The only' or 'only-begotten' is the *perfect* Son. John is building towards a specific identification. So far in this opening, he's revealed that the Logos is the Creator, is Life, is Light, is God and is with God, is with us. He's revealed that the Logos is the heavenly visitor who has tabernacled with us. But he has not yet identified Him by name.[84] He wants us to appreciate the transcendent majesty of the *'only Son'* before he tells us who He is. So he spelled out His perfection for us by using the Greek word, 'monogenes', which has a gematria of 496. It's a 'perfect' number. It speaks of the flawless brilliance of an immaculate jewel.

The effulgent cloud that engulfed the disciples on the Mount of Transfiguration, the visible glory of the Lord, caused them to fall facedown in terror. Their inability to stand is a reminder, not only of the gravitas of glory, but of events during the dedication of Solomon's Temple:

---

84 The verification that Jesus of Nazareth is the Word does not happen until verse 17.

> *When the priests left the Holy Place after setting the ark in place, the cloud filled the Lord's Temple so that the priests could not stand to minister because of the cloud, since the glory of the Lord filled the Lord's Temple.*
>
> 1 Kings 8:10–11^{ISV}

Glory is weighty. The Hebrew word for *glory* also means *honour* and has a sense of being substantial, significant, heavy. Although we don't directly associate honour with weight in English, we do have an indirect link. When we choose to dishonour someone or fail to pay them respect, we are said to treat them lightly, trivially or contemptuously.

In Scripture, the weight of divine glory made it difficult to remain standing. This is not an ordinary cloud, but one that pressed down awe and terror on those on whom it fell. John connected this glory to Christ dwelling among us. For contemporary Jews, this would have immediately evoked the concept of the *Shekhinah*. This is a term that does not appear in Scripture but is an important feature of rabbinic literature. *Shekhinah* means *dwelling* or *settling* and denotes the divine presence of God through the manifestation of a cloud of glory dwelling, settling or tabernacling in a particular place. It is no coincidence that it was the Feast of Tabernacles when Peter became confused and suggested putting up tents for Jesus, Moses and Elijah.

> *While he was still speaking, a bright cloud overshadowed them, and behold, a Voice from the cloud said, 'This is My beloved Son, with whom I am well pleased; listen to Him!'*
>
> Matthew 17:5^{NASB}

This is the moment when God tabernacled with His church. John testifies to the moment, to the wonder, the glory, the perfection, the loveliness, the grace. He is the witness whose word is faithful and true.

5.3 Death and Honour

> *Jesus said this to indicate the kind of death by which Peter would glorify God. And after He had said this, He told him, 'Follow Me.'*
>
> John 21:19[BSB]

IN BOTH THE HEBREW LANGUAGE as well as the Greek, the word for *glory* is also the word for *honour*. The two concepts are so deeply entwined as to be almost indistinguishable. So we might choose as an alternative translation:

> *Jesus said this to tell how Peter would die and bring honour to God. Then He said to Peter, 'Follow Me!'*
>
> John 21:19[CEV]

For Western thinkers, it's a struggle to perceive the relationship between death and honour—whereas the cultures of the East and Middle East understand them as intimately bound together.

Immediately after reporting this conversation between Jesus and Peter, the author of the gospel reminds us he is the disciple and the witness who testifies to the truth of these things. Likewise back at the beginning, immediately after mentioning the glory he has personally seen, the author mentions the testimony of John the Baptiser.

John [the Baptiser] *testified about Him.*	*This is the disciple who testifies to these things.*
John 1:15^{NASB}	John 21:24^{NIV}

Here we have, in a matching pair about glory-and-witness, the name of the author revealed. The disciple whom Jesus loved has set the scene so that he can be identified as someone named 'John'. He, like the other John—the Baptiser—is a witness whose *'testimony is true'*. (John 21:24^{NIV}) This is not an accidental placement. We can be sure of that when we consider later parallels featuring Mary the mother of Jesus and Mary Magdalene, Nicodemus and Nicodemus, Nathanael the doubter and Thomas the doubter as well as other matching scenes with more subtle counterparts.

John the apostle, John the Baptiser, Simon Peter are all here named as witnesses. The Greek word is *martyr*, and has come to be associated with witnessing unto death. From the very beginning of the Christian faith, a witness was one who risked their life to speak to the world of Jesus. A stand for truth, a stand for 'Jesus as Lord', a stand for the sanctity of all life and the value of all people in a culture where the paterfamilias could, with impunity, order the death of even adult children, a stand for the worth of every person in the face of the commodification of children and slaves—this was a hazardous business. To be a witness to Jesus and the values He espoused—to love God with all your heart and mind and soul and strength, and to love your neighbour as yourself—was a dangerous enterprise. Persecution was inevitable in the midst of the blessings, and death was a possibility.

John the Baptiser had died for his witness at the hands of Herod's executioner. Simon Peter too had died. John the apostle explains he doesn't know what the future holds: the words of Jesus about his own death—or deathlessness—were decidedly ambiguous.

5.4 Mathematics Became Man

It wasn't enough for John to spell out for the Gnostics that the Logos was grace and truth. That went without saying. The connotations of Logos, whether it related to word or number, reason or expression, were *good, true* and *beautiful.* Just another way, really, of saying *grace and truth.*

John started his revelation about the Logos being full of grace and truth with this shocking announcement: 'And the Word became flesh...' (John 1:14[ESV]) This was a horrifying idea for those Gnostics who believed the material world had been created as flawed and evil, not good. Its bentness in their view did not come from the entry of sin but was inherent in the very fabric of creation and the malevolence of the creator (who was not the Father but a malicious demi-urge). Flesh therefore was fundamentally corrupt. Only the spirit was good, and so the promise of resurrection was not one of a return to an ideal, glorified body but instead of a release from the body. To the Gnostics, 'resurrection' meant what anyone else would understand as 'death'.

Now Gnosticism had, and has, as many quirky different shades of belief as denominational Christianity does. John was specifically writing against the kind of Pythagorean Gnosticism promoted by Cerinthus—the man who caused him to grab his clothes and flee the public baths in Ephesus in case the wrath of God descended and the place turned into a cinder. Yet by the second century, John's anti-gnostic anti-Cerinthian message was considered by some believers to have been written by Cerinthus himself!

For Cerinthus, Jesus was the natural born son of Joseph and Mary who, as he grew up, became a holy man. At his baptism, he was invested with the 'Christ Spirit' and thereafter proclaimed the unknown Father. The Christ Spirit left Jesus at the resurrection, so Jesus the man died but the Christ Spirit remained 'impassible'.[85]

In clear defiance of this claim by Cerinthus that Jesus was flesh but Christ was spirit, John says that the *Word became flesh*. Perhaps because the mathematical design of his gospel shares much in common with Pythagorean mysticism, it would be possible to consider it was a Gnostic treatise for a few moments, but ultimately that unequivocal statement the *Word became flesh* also says *Mathematics became man*. Spirit has become corporeal. Expression has become embodied. Reason has inhabited a human form. The Ideal has taken on material existence. The Creator has become part of His creation. The Anointed One, the Christ, came into this world and lived and taught in downtown Galilee.

And, by the way, He was perfect. Not warped, not malevolent, not malicious, not corrupt, not bent. *Perfect*. Full of grace and truth. Good, true and beautiful. Who moreover created a cosmos that, reflecting His own nature, is also good, true and beautiful. But that has, unfortunately become defiled and debased through the ravages of sin.

This is John's account of the divine rescue mission accomplished by Jesus.

---

[85] Irenaeus, Bishop of Lugdunum, *Against Heresies (Book I, Chapter 26)*. Cerinthus' view was not the only Gnostic one: others thought that Christ only appeared to die. Instead Simon of Cyrene, the man conscripted by the Roman soldiers to carry the crossbeam for Him, was the one who was crucified while Christ stood amongst the bystanders laughing and mocking.

5.5 The Fire in the Equations

In *A Brief History of Time*, Stephen Hawking pondered the fact there is no particular reason our system of science and mathematics should actually work in any practical sense. How is it, he wondered, that the analytical systems we've created can actually predict the behaviour of electromagnetism, gravitational force, quantum mechanics or anything else for that matter? 'What is it,' he asked, 'that breathes fire into the equations and makes a universe for them to describe?'

Ask that question in the ancient classical world and there would have been a divide as wide as the chasm that exists today between science and religion. Moreover the ancient partition between the adherents of Pythagoreanism and Christianity persists into our own era.

Hawking might have felt that the fire in the equations was curious but it would not have been a mystery to the Pythagorean Brotherhood. The catechism called *On the Pythagorean Life* produced by Iamblichus, a third century philosopher, contained this teaching:

> Question: *What is the oracle of Delphi?*
> Answer: *The tetraktys. It is also the harmony in which the Sirens sing.*

So what is the tetraktys? What does it have to do with the sirens singing? Or the oracle at Delphi?

Now Iamblichus was trying to produce an ethical work on Pythagoreanism specifically aimed at undermining Christian moral teaching.[86] So, not surprisingly, the tetraktys[87] is a mathematical construction. The oracle at Delphi was dedicated to Python Apollo, the tutelary deity of the shrine who specialised in music, prophecy and healing. He had delegated the task of sustaining the universe to the sirens. Pythagoras was named after Python Apollo.

Although the pentagram is often said to be a symbol of the Pythagorean Brotherhood, its usage began quite late—about the second century. In the classical world, the ultimate mystical emblem of the Brotherhood was not the pentagram but the tetraktys: 10 dots arranged in a triangle.

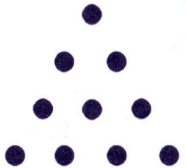

This iconic configuration was so sacred it was regarded as Manifest Deity, the source of nature, the Number of Numbers,

---

[86] After the Emperor Constantine died, his nephew Julian inherited a division of territory in the Roman Empire. Julian had turned his back on the Christianity of his youth and embraced Pythagorean theurgy. He wanted to overturn the Christianity introduced by his uncle but regarded this proposition as a difficult one, since he considered Constantine had basically bowed to the will of the people. He therefore decided that, to reinstate paganism, it was necessary to find an ethical and moral alternative to Christianity. Hence he encouraged the dissemination of *On the Pythagorean Life* by Iamblichus. Although the evidence for the symbolic meaning of 101 is therefore late, I nevertheless think the use of it in the gospels and epistles indicates it was understood the same way in the first century.

[87] Also spelled 'tetract'.

the Meaning of Meaning, the creative principle, the fundamental Truth of the universe, the heart of the Logos. Now, by Manifest Deity and heart of the Logos, there was not the slightest intention of pointing to Christ. Quite the opposite. Iamblichus was writing with the intent of establishing a rival to Christianity, not affirming its message. Hidden in his enigmatic answer about sirens, oracles and dot-arrangements is this extraordinary claim: Pythagoras[88] is the creator of the cosmos and, since the Sirens were supposed to sing one note each of the musical scale discovered by him, he is its sustainer as well via the Music of the Spheres.

In section 2.6, I noted that 101 is a number associated with the sustenance and maintenance of the universe. However, I didn't explain the reasons why at that point.

Let me set the background. There's a little known fact about stringed musical instruments that the Pythagoreans considered religiously significant. Now, it's almost universally said that, if one string is double the length of another, they will be an octave apart. That's a generalisation that's not quite accurate. Creating a perfect octave on a stringed instrument is *not* a matter of exactly doubling the length of the string. There is a tiny difference in size, equivalent to just over 101%, variously called in different time periods a 'Pythagorean comma' or 'diatonic comma'.

101 is a symbolic number that speaks to the Music of the Spheres and thus to the sustaining of the universe. And if you think it was restricted to the Pythagoreans, think again.

---

[88] As an apotheosis of either Pythian Apollo or Hyperborean Apollo. That is, just as Jesus was the incarnation of God Himself, Pythagoras was the incarnation or apotheosis of Apollo, the patron-god of music. Since the Music of the Spheres was understood as the essence of what sustained the universe then, according to Pythagorean understanding, Apollo was in charge of upholding, supporting and maintaining the universe.

Straight after the opening salutation comes Ephesians 1:3–14, which in Greek is a mammoth, convoluted 202-word sentence. Almost at the very end of the epistle is Ephesians 6:12–18 which describes the Armour of God in 101 words.

That 202-word sentence at the start is dominated by ideas about God sustaining the Christian. Let's take a look at one translation—which is considerably more than 202 words:

> *Blessed be the God and Father of our Lord Jesus Christ, who has blessed us in Christ with every spiritual blessing in the heavenly places, even as He chose us in Him before the foundation of the world, that we should be holy and blameless before Him. In love He predestined us for adoption to Himself as sons through Jesus Christ, according to the purpose of His will, to the praise of His glorious grace, with which He has blessed us in the Beloved. In Him we have redemption through His blood, the forgiveness of our trespasses, according to the riches of His grace, which He lavished upon us, in all wisdom and insight making known to us the mystery of His will, according to His purpose, which He set forth in Christ as a plan for the fullness of time, to unite all things in Him, things in heaven and things on earth.*
>
> *In Him we have obtained an inheritance, having been predestined according to the purpose of Him who works all things according to the counsel of His will, so that we who were the first to hope in Christ might be to the praise of His glory. In Him you also, when you heard the word of truth, the gospel of your salvation, and believed in Him, were sealed with the promised Holy Spirit, who is the guarantee of our inheritance until we acquire possession of it, to the praise of His glory.*[89]

---

89   English Standard Version

The passage opens with a triple reference to blessing: 'eulogos', made up of 'eu-', *good*, and '-logos', *word*. It's about being blessed by having good things spoken over us that we might prosper. While the passage does not mention 'sustenance' by name, it is implied throughout by the continued references to blessings, inheritance, riches, redemption.

The clincher for me, however, is the 101-word sequence describing the Armour of God. It's not simply 101 words long, the pattern of the words also happens to be arranged in a musical notation including the octave and perfect fifth. This is a knife-flick at the whole Pythagorean concept of music and worship.

That 202-word opening sentence is dominated by ideas about God blessing the Christian community. The Armour of God is about God protecting the Christian community. Blessing and protecting are about upholding, supporting, retaining, maintaining, sustaining.

Although Iamblichus wrote centuries later than either John or Paul, I believe the evidence is staring us right in the face: from the very earliest days of Christianity, the infiltration of Pythagorean-Platonism through the Gnostic influx meant that the very nature of the number system had to be carefully, repeatedly defined as created by God, not god in itself.

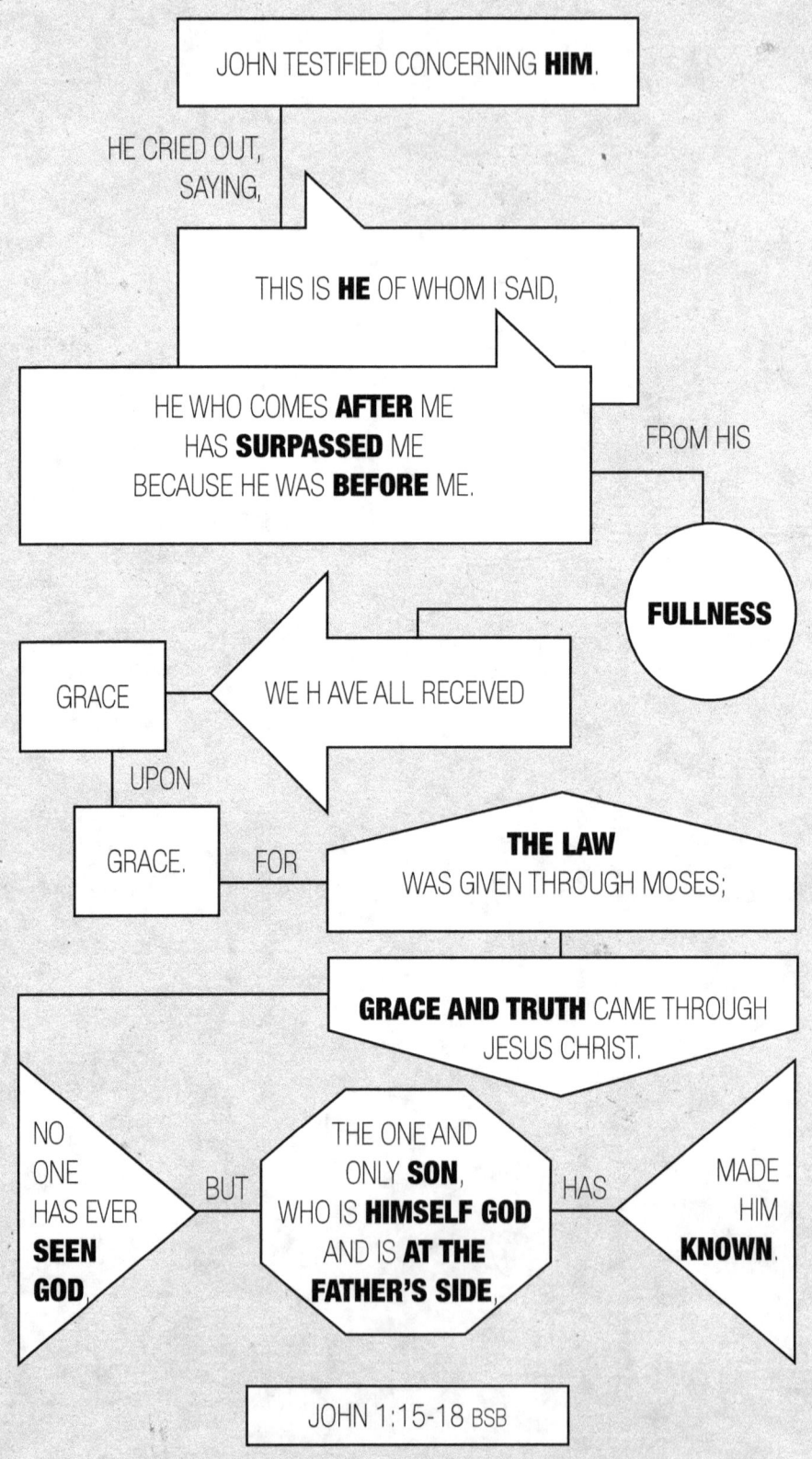

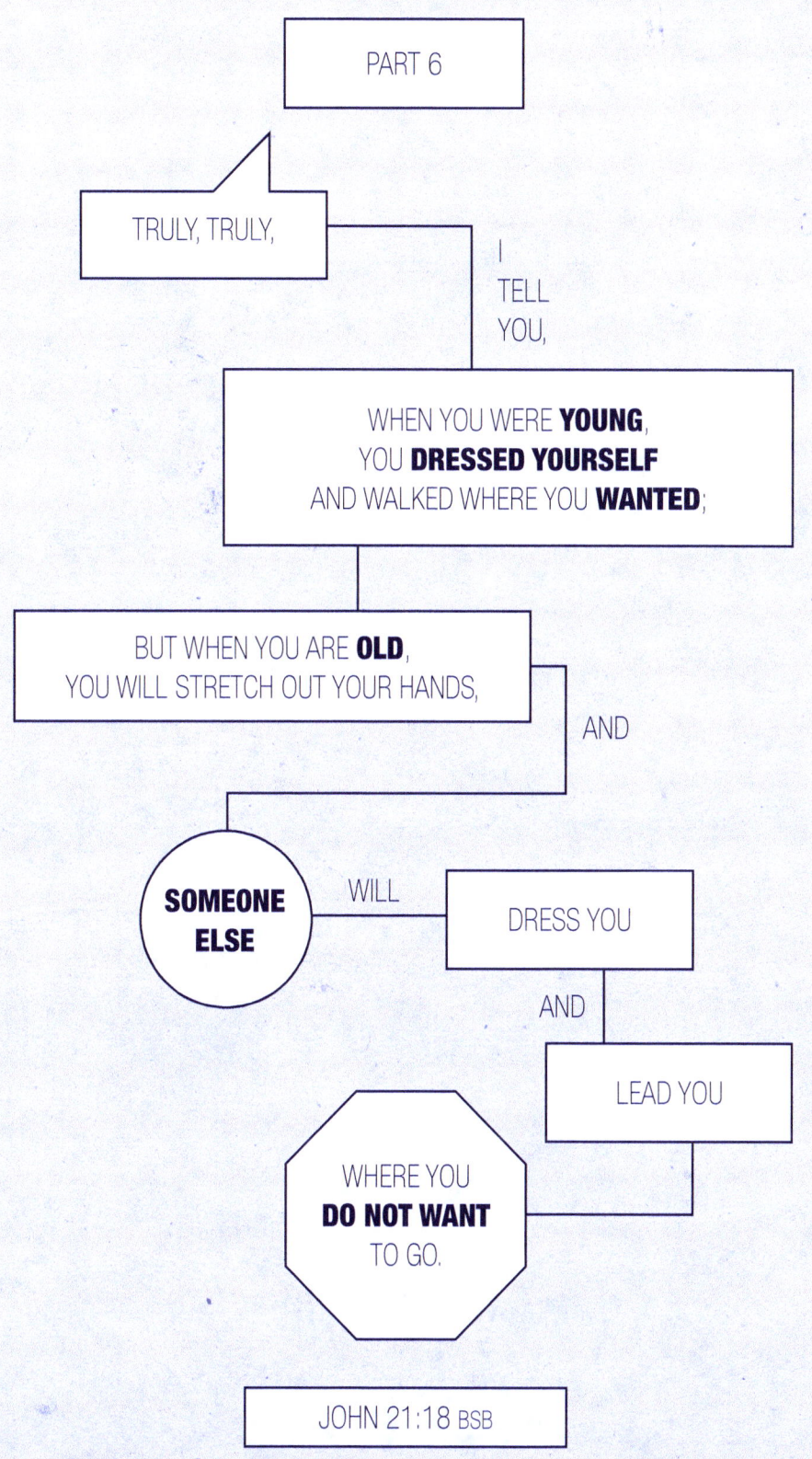

6.1 ENFOLDED BY GRACE

'AT THE FATHER'S SIDE': that's the description we have of Jesus. He is the Son full of grace and truth, the 'one and only' or 'only begotten'—that is, *monogenes*, with its embedded perfect number.

'At the Father's side' is a modernisation of an archaic phrase: *in the Father's bosom*. It's tempting to laugh at such outdated, awkward wording. Yet that would be to miss entirely the sense of tender warmth hidden within it. To be in someone's bosom meant to be tucked into a fold of a garment. It indicated a positioning that was close to the heart, and being held in place by pleats gathered together by the girdle.

This should remind us of the medieval conception of the universe—that the 'cosmos', from Greek *ornament*, was an exquisite jewelled decoration adorning the breast of the Father.

However the phrase, whether we think of it as 'at the Father's side' or 'in the Father's bosom', sheds a very different light on the comment about Peter's death. Each of John's chiastic elements informs its partner and is also informed by it. '*You dressed yourself,*' said Jesus, using the word for putting on a girdle or pulling up the slack on clothing with a belt. And then He says, '*someone else will dress you.*' In both cases He was referring to the action of creating the folds of a 'bosom'. And the parallelism suggests that, even in his death, Peter was safe in the Father's bosom, right there with Jesus, close to the heart of God. Caught up in the love-embrace of Father and Son, Peter glorified Them by honouring Them through his witness even unto death.

Peter is not alone, cradled in the bosom of God. John makes this very clear immediately after reporting the prophecy of Jesus about the death of Peter. He goes on to recall:

> *Having turned, Peter sees the disciple whom Jesus loved following, the one who also had reclined on His bosom at the supper and said, 'Lord, who is it who is betraying You?'*
>
> John 21:20^{BLB}

Most translations have words similar to 'leaned back against Him' rather than a more literal rendition of the Greek *'reclined on His bosom'*—a place of protection and affection. While John is very explicit in announcing that Jesus loved him in a special, tender way, he also declared that Peter—and, by extension, all the children of God—share that space.

Four times at the beginning John reiterates that Jesus is the grace-giver and grace-bringer—twice he couples grace with truth, and once he couples light with truth. Jesus is the One who surpasses John the Baptiser because, although He came after John, He was before him. He is the pre-eminent One who makes the Father—the Father who has never been seen—known to the children born of God. He not only presents us to the Father, He also presents the Father to us:

> *He is the radiance of His glory and the exact representation of His nature, and upholds all things by the word of His power.*
>
> Hebrews 1:3^{NASB}

Columba Marmion said, 'The Word, the Son, is essentially the glory of His Father. From all eternity, this Son… expresses the Father's perfection, and this is the essential glory that the Father receives. The Eternal Word is a Divine canticle singing the Father's praise… This is the infinite hymn that ever resounds in *sinu Patris* (in the bosom of the Father) and ever ravishes the Father. The Word is the Canticle that God inwardly sings to Himself, the Canticle that rises up from the depths of the Divinity, the Living Canticle wherein God eternally delights, because it is the infinite expression of His perfection.'[90]

---

[90] www.liturgyofthehours.org/post/blessed-columba-marmion-on-the-excellence-of-the-divine-office (accessed 10 November 2021)

6.2 Elijah's Mantle

Before John explicitly introduces a mention of Elijah, he prepares the way. The conversation at the end of the gospel about dressing (including the mention in John 21:7 of Peter putting on his outer garment) explicitly signifies honour and glory. Yet there are more subtle overtones in this scene that resonate both with the tabernacling of Jesus among us and with the legacy of Elijah.

The Greek word for the *wrapping, coat* or *mantle* that Peter dons before he jumps out of the boat in the last scene of John's gospel is 'ependutés'. It is derived from 'ependuomai', and that refers to the glorified body in which Jesus clothes each believer at His return. Paul uses the word twice in his second letter to the Corinthians, as emphasised:

> *We know that if our earthly house, this tent, is destroyed, we have a building from God, a house not made with hands, eternal in the heavens. For in this we groan, earnestly desiring to be* **clothed** *with our habitation which is from heaven, if indeed, having been clothed,*[91] *we shall not be found naked. For we who are in this tent groan, being burdened, not because we want to be unclothed, but further* **clothed**, *that mortality may be swallowed up by life.*
>
> 2 Corinthians 5:1–4[NKJV]

---

[91] The word here is slightly different: 'enduo' has the sense of *being invested with clothing*. That has a resonance of a ceremonial act of dressing, not simply slapping on radiantly white clothes.

This glorified body that Jesus wraps us in and enfolds around us is both holy clothing and sacred tabernacle. Just as the glory of the divine cloud, the Shekhinah of God, rested upon the tabernacle sanctuary during the wilderness wanderings, so the glory of Jesus was manifest for Peter, James and John during the Feast of Tabernacles on the Mount of Transfiguration. John testified to this when he said, *'We have seen His glory,'* but now he presents this glory as a promise to all believers.

Peter may have inherited Elijah's mantle—given to him by Jesus—as the final episode in the gospel proclaims but this is not for Peter alone. It is for all of us.

6.3 Out in the Wilderness

Before looking at the next scene in the fourth gospel, where the priests and Levites from Jerusalem confront John the Baptiser, I want to examine an event he does not describe.

As John moves past the prologue to his gospel and into the narrative, he drops some important clues about the dates. Three times John records *'the next day'* (John 1:29, 35, 43) before mentioning *'on the third day'* right at the start of what we have designated the second chapter. Now many commentators think *'the third day'* simply means Tuesday, the third day of the Hebrew week. However, I believe it's a hint about chronology and, if we can interpret the clues, we can identify the season when all these events take place. Instead of 'Tuesday', I believe that, by saying *'the next day'*, *'the next day'*, *'the next day'* and *'on the third day'*, John was revealing that six days elapsed. It was just under a week from the time John the Baptiser answered the interrogators from Jerusalem until the wedding feast at Cana. But the fact that it's precisely *six* days is important: with this information plus some other clues we should be able to figure out that the first scene happens on the Day of Atonement and the wedding begins at the Feast of Tabernacles.

Since Jesus, rather strangely, didn't turn up until *the day after* Yom Kippur—the Day of Atonement—we might ask ourselves where

He was and what He was doing. It surely would have been far more logical for Him to be at the baptismal site at Bethany-beyond-the-Jordan on Yom Kippur. What could be more important than repentance on such a Day?

Personally I think that Jesus was very busy on Yom Kippur that year: He was in a face-off with the satan somewhere out in the wilderness beyond the Jordan. This, I believe, was the day of temptation, the day when He was tested three times by the devil. It was the last of forty days that He spent fasting and praying—indicating that He would have started on the first day of the month of Elul. This time period through to Yom Kippur exactly matches the customary forty days of Teshuvah, *repentance*, which commemorates the season when Moses ascended Mount Sinai for the third time, there to receive a new set of stone tablets to replace the one broken when he threw them down on seeing the golden calf. The baptism of Jesus would therefore have taken place on the first of Elul, the beginning of the season of repentance.[92]

Yom Kippur, besides being the Day of Atonement, was the day Moses descended the mountain with the second pair of stone tablets with the commandments on them.

That suggests the interchange between Jesus and the devil about stones, bread and the Word of God has much deeper and more profound undertones. The temptation to change stones to bread is charged with the notion of modifying God's commandments into something practical and useful for the present moment and current needs. It might seem, on the surface, that it wouldn't be breaking any divine law to change stones into bread, but there is a deep spiritual principle involved. Transforming stones into bread

---

92   1 Elul is also the start of 'Yemei Ratzon', *Days of Favour*. The *Days of Favour* refers to God's lovingkindness and forgiveness in making and inscribing the commandments on a new set of sapphire plates for Moses during this forty-day period.

involves a change of *kind*. It's magic. To change bread into bread, such as happened during the multiplication of the loaves and fishes, is NOT a change of *kind*. It's a miracle that reflects a similar generative power to that of one seed of grain being planted and becoming many seeds of grain at harvest time.

To change stones into bread would be to use the creative power that God put into words and into His Word against Him. That's the simplest definition of magic that I know. Miracles use God's power in accord with His purposes but magic uses His power to defy Him.

John's gospel is full of 'signs': we might call them *miracles* but he referred to them as *signs*.[93] John obviously hoped to change his readers' perception of miraculous power from the Wonder-Worker towards Jesus as a signpost to God Himself. 'No one has ever seen God, but the one and only Son, who is Himself God and is at the Father's side, has made Him known.' John tried to change the focus from the marvel, the wonder and the demonstration of power and even point beyond Jesus to the Father.

After the first temptation, the devil takes Jesus to the pinnacle of the Temple.[94] Have you ever wondered why it's the Temple? Remember, this is Yom Kippur, the Day of Atonement. That was the only time during the year the High Priest could enter the Holy of Holies and approach the Ark of the Covenant to sprinkle the blood of sacrifice on the mercy-seat, *kaphar*, 'atoning cover'.[95] Also within the Temple was the 'eben ha-shetiyah', *the stone from which the world was woven*, the foundation stone representing the cornerstone of the entire created cosmos.

---

93 The question of how many signs there are is an open one. Many writers say seven, but Charles Welch makes a good case for eight. See: *The Eight Signs in John's Gospel – Appendix to the Companion Bible* levendwater.org/companion/append176.html (accessed 14 October 2021)

94 Whether this is the second or third temptation is not clear.

95 'Kaphar' and 'kippur' are related words.

'Well,' says the devil, 'I'll take Your line from Deuteronomy, *"Man does not live on bread alone but on every breath that comes from the mouth of God"*[96] and I'll raise You Psalm 91, *"He will command His angels concerning you to guard you in all your ways. On their hands they will bear you up, lest you strike your foot against a stone."* Yeah, yeah, sure You can quote the Torah like a good boy reciting his memory verses but that doesn't prove You really believe it. How about throwing Yourself down from this height to show You really have faith in God?'

Now, bearing in mind the Temple contains both the mercy-seat and the Foundation Stone, the replica of the cornerstone of creation, then leaping over either of them is basically the same as accepting threshold covenant. Instead of a 'pass over' at God's invitation, this would have been a 'pass over' at the devil's behest and would have brought Jesus into covenant with the Prince of this World. If Jesus had failed this test, the consequences would have been catastrophic. Adam's disloyalty to God had given the devil the rights to the earth; if Jesus had been disloyal, it would have meant the entire universe would have been handed over to the rule of the satan.

As for the 'high mountain' where the devil showed Jesus all the kingdoms of this world, I have to suspect Jesus returned to this same 'high mountain' three years and six days later. At that time the glory of the kingdoms of this world were shown up as tawdry and gaudy by the overshadowing and majestic glory of the Father at the Transfiguration.

---

96   Deuteronomy 8:3[BSB]

6.4 On Top of the Temple

IN THE TIME OF JESUS, PSALM 91 was seen as a protective talisman against the powers of evil. Not too much has changed in the last few millennia because I know believers who recite it each day as part of their spiritual defence routine.

The satan clearly laughs at this kind of attitude. By quoting the psalm to Jesus, he was indicating that he was completely unperturbed by it. As far as he was concerned, it didn't matter if anyone tried to use it against him. He could airily and jauntily say it himself. It's not the psalm that protects us—it's our covenant defender. If we put our faith in words rather than the Word, we're in trouble.

Now there was a particular inbuilt trick in this test. One part of the calling of Jesus was to be a rabbi. He was a teacher as well as a healer and redeemer. We can't shave off one part and treat it as irrelevant—as many people tend to do. Some believers ignore the teacher, some ignore the healer and some the redeemer—deciding that the particular aspect they're side-lining is not for current times.

By quoting a psalm, the satan challenged the teaching aspect of Jesus' calling by using a very fine example of traditional rabbinic technique. It was intended to create a double-bind, and it was incredibly subtle in the way it was presented. For Jesus, it was no longer a matter of just saying 'no' to the devil; a lot depended on *how* He said 'no'.

This is a diabolic trap. It would have been so easy for Jesus to go straight to the next verse of Psalm 91 and identify the satan on that basis, perhaps even launch a defence using that as a starting point. That would have been taking the bait and falling straight into the snare. Because that was the way a student would respond to a teacher. Thus Jesus would have technically been accepting the devil's implied offer, his infernal proposal that: 'I'll be Your rabbi, Your mentor, Your counsellor, Your teacher.'

In many respects, it didn't really matter if Jesus jumped from the pinnacle of the Temple or not if He came back with any part of Psalm 91.

However, He was wise enough to respond with: *'Do not put the Lord your God to the test,'* from Deuteronomy 6:16. It's important to note He made a selection here. The full verse is: *'Do not test the Lord your God as you tested Him at Massah.'*

It's not a flat-out prohibition: *don't ever test God*. There are in fact times when God actually invites us to test Him.

There's the well-known verse from Malachi, where God says to His people, *'Test Me in this.'*[97] And there's the prophet Isaiah who, after God had spoken to King Ahaz, telling him to ask for a sign, seriously rebuked the king for what seemed like a pious royal response: *'I will not put the Lord to the test.'*[98]

So clearly it's not simply a matter of quoting Scripture so the devil will flee. Some people think that, if we know the Word well enough, spiritual warfare will mean dipping into the arsenal of

---

97   Malachi 3:10
98   Isaiah 7:12

Scripture for the nearest weapon. But, as Jesus shows, we have to be in relationship with the Father and so deeply dependent on the Holy Spirit that we know *which* verse to apply *when*.

The Day of Atonement is immensely significant timing as far as the temptation of Jesus is concerned. I think it's possible to actually pinpoint the precise minute of this temptation. To begin with, Jesus was out in the wilderness—driven out there, just like the scapegoat would be on this most solemn of days. From the desert on the far side of the Jordan, the devil whisked Him to the very top of the Temple in Jerusalem. After this slick act of translocation, the devil makes his challenge:

> 'If You are the Son of God… throw Yourself down. For it is written:
> He will command His angels concerning You,
> and they will lift You up in their hands,
> so that You will not strike your foot against a stone.'
>
> Matthew 4:6^{BSB}

The satan was undoubtedly intent on complete and total ruination of Jesus' calling. So the most critical moment to kill it, right at the outset, would be just after the high priest had entered the Holy of Holies to sprinkle blood on the mercy-seat covering the Ark of the Covenant.

Right after that, someone leaping across—*passing over*—the mercy-seat, the 'kapporeth' or *place of atonement*, would wreck that act of petition to God for the purification of the nation. Only if God asked Jesus to do it would it be fine—because it would have been a covenantal invitation by the Father. But because it was the satan who was asking Jesus to leap over the blood-stained cornerstone, a threshold covenant would have been enacted between the pair of them instead.

Had Jesus actually jumped, He would have *passed over* the earthly counterpart of the cornerstone of the entire universe. And because covenant involves exchange, the most dire outcome would have come to pass.

When Adam was tempted and lured into acquiescing with the serpent, he lost his regency of the world. It passed into the possession of the prince of the power of the air, the spirit who rules the sons of disobedience. Had Christ actually jumped—and there is no question He would have had to have been genuinely tempted to, otherwise there was no point to the test—He would have handed over the dominion of the entire cosmos to the enemy. The first Adam succumbed and lost the earth; the second Adam would have, had He succumbed, lost the heavens as well.

The satan's ambition hadn't changed at all. He still wanted the throne of God. And getting Jesus to jump would have been a short-cut to taking possession of it.

PART

And this was John's testimony when the Jews of Jerusalem sent priests and Levites to ask him, 'Who are you?'

He did not refuse to confess, but openly declared, 'I am not the Christ.'

'Then who are you?' they inquired.

'Are you Elijah?'

He said, 'I am not.'

'Are you the Prophet?'

He answered, 'No.'

So they said to him, 'Who are you? We need an answer for those who sent us. What do you say about yourself?'

John replied in the words of Isaiah the prophet: 'I am a voice of one calling in the wilderness, "Make straight the way for the Lord."'

John 1:19–23 BSB

VII

So when they had eaten breakfast, Jesus said to Simon Peter, 'Simon, son of Jonah, do you love me more than these?' He said to him, 'Yes, Lord; you know that I love you.' He said to him, 'Feed my lambs.' He said to him again a second time, 'Simon, son of Jonah, do you love me?' He said to him, 'Yes, Lord; you know that I love you.' He said to him, 'Tend my sheep.' He said to him the third time, 'Simon, son of Jonah, do you love me?' Peter was grieved because he said to him the third time, 'Do you love me?' And he said to him, 'Lord, you know all things; you know that I love you.' Jesus said to him, 'Feed my sheep.'

John 21:15-17 NKJV

7.1 The Four Craftsmen

IN THE TIME OF JESUS, the Jewish people were looking forward to the fulfillment of many promises that God had made through His prophets across the ages. Moses had proclaimed:

> 'The Lord your God will raise up for you a prophet like me from among you, from your fellow Israelites. You must listen to him.'
>
> Deuteronomy 18:15^{NIV}

There was an expectation that this Prophet would be like Moses, and thus a national deliverer, a messiah. The people of Israel, suffering under the yoke of the Romans, did not so much anticipate THE messiah as a set of them. Based on the prophecy of Zechariah, they understood that God would send four agents of redemption[99] to His people to unseat the powers of the nations who held the people of Israel captive.

> Then the Lord showed me four craftsmen.
>
> I asked, 'What are they going to do?'

---

99 ffoz.org/discover/prophecy/the-four-craftsmen-agents-of-redemption.html (accessed 16 November 2021)

> *He answered, 'Those horns scattered Judah so widely that no one could lift up his head. But the craftsmen have come to terrify them, to throw down the horns of the nations.'*
>
> Zechariah 1:20–21^{GWT}

A long-standing tradition[100] about the 'Four Craftsmen' interpreted them as:

- Messiah, son of David
- Messiah, son of Joseph
- The Righteous Priest
- Elijah

There would be a royal messiah, a war messiah, a priestly messiah and the Elijah-who-was-to-come. Messiah, son of David, would be the king who would usher in a golden reign after Messiah, son of Joseph, the war commander, was killed in a cataclysmic battle that would see all of Israel's enemies destroyed and swept away.

In his gospel, John twice uses *'Son of Joseph'* as a title for Jesus where the other evangelists restrict that term entirely to the genealogies. On the other hand, John does not use 'Son of David' at all where it is common in the other gospels. Matthew, Mark and Luke present the theme of the kingly messiah, but John reveals the war messiah, the one who followed in the footsteps of the warrior-leader, Hoshea, who had been renamed Joshua by Moses.

The national yearning of Israel was that 'the Prophet' would be Moses returned, the 'Righteous Priest' would be Melchizedek returned, and the 'Elijah-to-come' would be Elijah returned. The people looked forward to the completion of the last words of the prophecy of Malachi:

---

100 See *Sukkah* 52b of the Talmud.

> *Behold, I am going to send you Elijah the prophet before the coming of the great and terrible day of the Lord. He will turn the hearts of the fathers to their children, and the hearts of the children to their fathers... so that I will not come and strike the land with a curse.*
>
> Malachi 4:5–6[AMP]

No one expected all four craftsmen to be the same person. Even today we tend to think of three of the four applying to Jesus, while considering the last to be John the Baptiser. In fact, even the Elijah aspect of this tradition applies more closely to Jesus than it ever did to His cousin John.

7.2 Three questions by the water

W‍HILE JESUS WAS OUT IN THE DESERT being challenged three times by the devil, John the Baptiser was back at Bethany-beyond-the-Jordan also being challenged. 'Who are you?' he was asked three times by messengers from the leaders in Jerusalem.

Three times he denies a specific identification: he is *not* the Christ, he is *not* Elijah, he is *not* the Prophet.

He is *not* the Christ—that is, he is not the anointed one, and therefore he was not royal messiah nor the war messiah.

He is *not* Elijah—that is, he is not the one Malachi prophesied would turn the hearts of parents and children towards each other in genuine repentance.

He is *not* the Prophet—that is, he is not Moses returned.

Jesus, of course, later identified John as the Elijah-who-was-to-come. He did so just after the Transfiguration when He was descending the mountain with Peter, James and John.[101] Their minds still processing the event and the unexpected appearance of Moses and Elijah, they asked Him:

> *'Why do the teachers of religious law insist that Elijah must return before the Messiah comes?'*
>
> *Jesus replied, 'Elijah is indeed coming first to get everything ready. But I tell you, Elijah has already come, but he wasn't recognised, and they chose to abuse him. And in the same way they will also make the Son of Man suffer.'*
>
> *Then the disciples realised He was talking about John the Baptist.*
>
> Matthew 17:10–13^{NLT}

Regardless of Jesus' words, however, it is plain the Baptiser did not see himself as the one who would fulfill Malachi's prophecy or be the one to bring to pass all that Elijah had left undone. In that self-assessment, he was indeed correct. He did not complete the unfinished work of Elijah. That was left to Jesus.

Nevertheless, it is readily apparent why the people at the time should have, and indeed obviously did, suspect the Baptiser was the Elijah-who-was-to-come. Both John and Elijah were notable

---

101 In the gospels, questions of identity often occur over the season of Yom Kippur, the Day of Atonement, and Sukkot, the Feast of Tabernacles. Dwight Pryor, *Jesus—The Fullness of Tanakh*, in John Fieldsend (ed.), Clifford Hill (ed.), Walter Riggans (ed.), John C.P. Smith (ed.), Fred Wright (ed.), *Roots and Branches: Explorations in the Jewish Context of the Christian Faith*, PVM Trust 1998, points out that, just a few days prior to the Transfiguration, Jesus had asked His disciples who people thought He was and also who they thought He was. Several answers are given—but God's answer to Jesus' question is not revealed until the Transfiguration itself. God's statement is a combination of phrases from the Law (Moses), the Prophets (Isaiah) and the sacred writings (Psalms). In addition, there are three witnesses to the Father's words, reflecting this same threefold division of Law, Prophets and sacred writings: Moses, Elijah and the Father Himself.

for their calls for repentance, both of them ministered in Samaria and Gilead, both of them were associated with the same locality where a brook flowed in the Jordan.[102] Both of them wore strange, signature clothing of hair and leather belts,[103] both of them ran afoul of a woman who was married to a ruler of Samaria,[104] both of them were able to talk companionably to that ruler even while they were confronting him about his sins. In addition, both of them had a mission to proclaim the coming king,[105] both of them saw heaven opened and a symbol of the Holy Spirit descending from above.[106]

John the apostle, the writer of the fourth gospel, paralleled the opening three questions about the identity of John the Baptiser with the three questions put to Simon, son of John, in his concluding section.

---

[102] Elijah began his ministry, then went immediately to the Brook Cherith where he was fed by ravens. This was later to become the location of Bethany-beyond-the-Jordan where John was first baptising before he moved to Aenon near Salim in Samaria. Elijah's hometown of Tishbe is thought by some commentators to be another name for Jabesh Gilead—one meaning of Jabesh is *sorrow*. In a strong parallel, one meaning of Bethany-beyond-the-Jordan is *house of sorrow beyond the Jordan*.

[103] Elijah was either hairy or wore clothing of hair with a leather belt. This description was sufficient for King Ahaziah to immediately identify him from a report. (2 Kings 1:8) John wore camel's hair garments with a leather belt. (Matthew 3:4; Mark 1:6)

[104] In Elijah's case this was Jezebel, wife of Ahab, and in John's case it was Herodias, wife of Herod Antipas. Herod enjoyed talking to John; and Elijah, while greatly afraid of Jezebel, was not only was able to confront Ahab but actually lead him to repentance.

[105] Elijah was tasked with anointing Hazael as king of Aram to replace Ben-Hadad. He did not do this. His servant Elisha later told Hazael he would be king but it is not recorded he anointed him. Elijah was also appointed to anoint Jehu as king of Samaria to replace Ahab—another mission he never completed, despite the opportunity to do so. John, of course, did complete the proclamation of the coming King.

[106] Elijah saw fire descend from heaven; John saw a dove descend from heaven.

In both cases, they are questions about identity. The questions put to the Baptiser should remind us of an incident, exactly three years later,[107] that took place in the north of Israel.

> *When Jesus came to the region of Caesarea Philippi, He questioned His disciples: 'Who do people say the Son of Man is?'*
>
> *They replied, 'Some say John the Baptist; others say Elijah; and still others, Jeremiah or one of the prophets.'*
>
> *'But what about you?' Jesus asked. 'Who do you say I am?'*
>
> *Simon Peter answered, 'You are the Christ, the Son of the living God.'*
>
> Matthew 16:13–16^{BSB}

Once again, it's Yom Kippur, the Day of Atonement. Once again, Elijah and the prophets, as well as the Christ are all mentioned. Once again, the question of identity and its associated calling are raised.

This emphasis on identity helps us to understand the episode involving Simon Peter at the end of John's gospel. Although the breakfast by the lake does not take place on Yom Kippur, its chiastic placement informs us that this too is about identity and destiny.

The breakfast Jesus cooked for Simon Peter and the other disciples was bread baked on hot coals along with fish. There is only one other breakfast of bread baked on hot coals mentioned in Scripture:

> *Then he lay down and slept under the broom tree. Suddenly, an angel touched him. The angel told him, 'Get up and eat.' Then he looked, and there at his head was a loaf of bread baked over hot stones, and a jug of water. So he ate and*

---

[107] By the Hebrew luni-solar calendar, not our modern solar calendar.

> *drank and lay down again. Then the angel of the Lord returned for a second time and touched him. He said, 'Get up and eat, or the journey will be too much for you.' So he got up, ate, and drank. Then on the strength from that food, he walked forty days and forty nights to Horeb, the mountain of God.*
>
> 1 Kings 19:5–8^{HCSB}

This breakfast happened when Elijah was on the run from Jezebel. He'd abandoned his calling, decided he couldn't take it anymore and turned his back on life as a 'Man of God'. Simon Peter was in similar circumstances. He'd abandoned his calling, decided he couldn't take it anymore and turned his back on life as a 'Follower of Jesus'. He just wanted to retire and take up his old profession as a fisherman. No more of this 'fisher of men' business. Just catching fish, not hauling in people.

It was a pivotal moment. Just as it was for Elijah under the broom tree. The food provided by the angel there was not sustenance to enable him to travel down to the mountain at Sinai. Rather it was divine provision and fortification to turn around, face Jezebel and her threats, and bring down her government. But Elijah chose not to pursue that course of action: he deserted his calling and never completed the tasks God later asked of him—to anoint Jehu and Hazael.

The breakfast when Peter was questioned by Jesus was at a similar critical juncture. When Peter said to his fellow disciples that he was going fishing, he wasn't talking about a nostalgic boat ride across the Sea of Galilee with a spot of recreational fishing on the side. He meant it was all over for him as far as following Jesus was concerned. He was intending to go out for an all-nighter, and take up where he left off before Jesus upended his life.

Now the three questions posed to him by the lakeside reflect the questions posed to the Baptiser. That's what their positioning is designed to do. But that's not the first thing that would spring to any reader's mind as they saw this story. The interrogation Peter had endured in the courtyard of the High Priest, Caiaphas, is much more likely to be foremost in anyone's thoughts. The comparisons are plain: both happened in the early morning, both happened at a fireside, both involved a set of three questions.

> Peter stood outside at the door. Then the disciple who was known to the high priest went out and spoke to the doorkeeper, and brought Peter in.
>
> At this, the servant girl watching the door said to Peter, 'Aren't you also one of this man's disciples?'
>
> 'I am not,' he answered.
>
> Because it was cold, the servants and officers were standing around a charcoal fire they had made to keep warm. And Peter was also standing with them, warming himself...
>
> So they asked him, 'Aren't you also one of His disciples?'
>
> He denied it and said, 'I am not.'
>
> One of the high priest's servants, a relative of the man whose ear Peter had cut off, asked, 'Didn't I see you with Him in the garden?'
>
> Peter denied it once more, and immediately a rooster crowed.
>
> John 18:16–27^{BSB}

In denying Jesus, Peter was forsaking his own identity. He was turning his back on 'Cephas', *cornerstone*, and trying desperately to slip back into the role of Simon, the impetuous Galilean fisherman who had never met rabbi Jesus. Yet even that understanding of himself was under immense threat. Jesus had warned him that the satan had asked to test all the disciples and sift them to the point of overthrow. But apparently it was not 'Cephas' that the satan had wanted to winnow in the sieve. He wanted to toss 'Simon' up and down repeatedly:

> *Simon, Simon, listen! Satan has demanded to have you apostles for himself. He wants to separate you from Me as a farmer separates wheat from husks.*
>
> Luke 22:31^{GWT}

Moreover, when Jesus later restored Peter during the breakfast by the water, He did not use the name 'Cephas' or 'Peter'. Three times Jesus called him, 'Simon son of John.' Three times Jesus talks about sheep, not fish.

John the apostle indicates he personally witnessed these three questions. He also hints he was present when John the Baptiser was presented with three questions. In each case, the questions were not only about a specific calling, but a calling defined in relation to Jesus. For John the Baptiser, he was the Voice announcing the coming of the Lamb of God; for Simon Peter, he was the Under-Shepherd charged with providing nurture for the lambs and sheep of the flock.

The comment of Jesus that follows this re-instatement, *'When you are old you will stretch out your hands, and someone else will dress you and lead you where you do not want to go,'* is not simply a prophecy of martyrdom. It is another back-link to the Baptiser, a man who also paid the price for heralding the coming of the Kingdom of God.

The theme of 'three questions' thus forms a flow connecting the prophet Elijah and his first-century successors—initially John the Baptiser, then later Simon Peter, appointed by Jesus to shepherd His flock.

7.3 Elijah's Unfinished Task

The life of Jesus forms a running commentary on the history of Israel. His words are few but He didn't pull any punches with His actions. The dark flaws of Scripture's heroes were laid bare as Jesus picked up the ripped tapestry they left behind them and began to mend it with immense insight and loving care. The status of Elijah, even now, is so high he is effectively idolised—to the point where his dereliction of his prophetic office goes virtually unnoticed.

Elijah burst onto the scene in the First Book of Kings without any preamble. He told King Ahab of Samaria that not a single drop of rain was going to fall on the land until he—Elijah—said so. Then he took off for the brook Cherith, hid there for a season until the pools dried up, before heading for Zarephath where he was fed by a widow. Three and a half years after his first prophetic announcement he returned to Samaria to confront the spiritual forces behind Ahab's throne in a climactic face-off with the prophets of Baal and Asherah.

Just before that happened, Elijah met with Ahab's steward Obadiah.

> *As Obadiah went on his way, Elijah suddenly met him. When Obadiah recognised him, he fell facedown and said, 'Is it you, my lord Elijah?'*
>
> *'It is I,' he answered. 'Go tell your master, "Elijah is here!"'*
>
> *But Obadiah replied, 'How have I sinned, that you are handing your servant over to Ahab to put me to death?… I do not know where the Spirit of the Lord may carry you off when I leave you. Then when I go and tell Ahab and he does not find you, he will kill me. But I, your servant, have feared the Lord from my youth. Was it not reported to my lord what I did when Jezebel slaughtered the prophets of the Lord? I hid a hundred prophets of the Lord, fifty men per cave, and I provided them with food and water. And now you say, "Go tell your lord that Elijah is here!" He will kill me!'*
>
> *Then Elijah said, 'As surely as the Lord of Hosts lives, before whom I stand, I will present myself to Ahab today.'*
>
> 1 Kings 18:7–15^{BSB}

After this, Obadiah went off and arranged the meeting. The king, the people and the prophets of Baal and Asherah gathered on Mount Carmel. At the beginning of the contest, Elijah makes this statement:

> *'I am the only remaining prophet of the Lord.'*
>
> 1 Kings 18:22^{ESV}

An interesting comment in the light of Obadiah's statement about the hundred prophets holed up in two caves. Did Elijah forget? Or was this a sliver of pride showing up? Was he was saying that the prophets Obadiah had hidden didn't really count?

This remark about being the only remaining prophet is one he eventually makes three times in total.

God says to him after he's fled down to Horeb and spent a night in a cave:

> *'What are you doing here, Elijah?'*
>
> *'I have been very zealous for the Lord, the God of Hosts,' he replied, 'but the Israelites have forsaken Your covenant, torn down Your altars, and killed Your prophets with the sword. I am the only one left, and they are seeking my life as well.'*

1 Kings 19:10^{BSB}

God then basically asked Elijah to reconsider. He sent wind, earthquake, fire—and ultimately became present in the still, small voice, before repeating exactly the same question: *'What are you doing here, Elijah?'*

This is very much what Jesus asked Peter by the lake. He was effectively saying: 'What are you doing here, Simon?' That story—wonderfully—has a very different outcome from Elijah's story.

Because Elijah, on being asked what a second time, gave God word-for-word, an identical answer:

> *'I have been very zealous for the Lord, the God of Hosts,' he replied, 'but the Israelites have forsaken Your covenant, torn down Your altars, and killed Your prophets with the sword. I am the only one left, and they are seeking my life as well.'*

1 Kings 19:13–14^{BSB}

I am the only one left. That's not only *not* true, Elijah should know it's not. Even the shaking of God was insufficient for Elijah to remember the truth. He had become so complicit with the spirit of panic, as well as the spirit of forgetting, that their hold on his life actually destroyed his calling.

So God essentially told Elijah he could retire.

> 'Go back by the way you came, and go to the Desert of Damascus. When you arrive, you are to anoint Hazael as king over Aram. You are also to anoint Jehu… as king over Israel and Elisha… to succeed you as prophet.'

And at the end of His speech, God delivers a 'by the way' when He says:

> 'I have reserved seven thousand in Israel—all whose knees have not bowed to Baal and whose mouths have not kissed him.'
>
> 1 Kings 19:15-17^{BSB}

In the next chapter, it becomes clear how wrong Elijah was when he said three times, 'I am the only one left.' Various prophets advise and admonish King Ahab during the wars between Samaria and Aram.

Now God had given Elijah one last task before retirement—to change the government.

When Elijah had finished his work on Mount Carmel, I believe his next task should have been to call on Obadiah to usher the hundred prophets of Yahweh out of the caves and take over the governmental positions previously occupied by the prophets of Baal and Asherah. There are interesting clues to follow—mathematical clues, of course!—that suggest this was what God had in mind. He wanted a complete palace revolution that would overturn the culture of death worship fostered by Jezebel.

But it required a particular timing. It had to be done within a few days or it would be too late. By the time Elijah had fled from Jezebel as far as Beersheba, six days had passed and the opportunity was on the cusp of being lost. The breakfast provided by the angel at this point was not to give Elijah the strength to go on—but to go back.

But once he had run south for forty more days and would have needed another seven weeks or so to return, the time was no longer right. So, at Horeb, God gave Elijah 'Plan B' for governmental change: anoint Hazael, anoint Jehu and anoint Elisha.

Perhaps Elijah anointed Elisha. He threw his mantle over him. But he certainly didn't ever anoint Jehu or Hazael.

He forgot. At least I hope he forgot. Because the other option is open defiance of God.

We know that Elijah either forgot or defied God because of something Jehu said. Years later, he was finally anointed by one of the sons of the prophets. Taking off in his chariot, driving like a madman, he met King Joram and King Ahaziah on the plot of ground that had once been Naboth's vineyard. Joram was killed there, and Jehu said to his officer Bidkar:

> 'Remember how you and I were riding together in chariots behind Ahab ... when the Lord spoke this prophecy against him: "Yesterday I saw the blood of Naboth and the blood of his sons, declares the Lord, and I will surely make you pay for it on this plot of ground."'
>
> 2 Kings 9:25-26[BSB]

Now, the person who delivered this prophecy to Ahab was Elijah. Jehu's speech to Bidkar tells us that Elijah didn't just meet up with Ahab, he also met up with Jehu. And he did not take—or arrange—the opportunity to obey the Lord and anoint Jehu as Ahab's successor. The evil that Ahab did and continued to do was, in part, Elijah's responsibility because he either forgot to obey God or else he decided that God had chosen the wrong candidate.

Jehu was manic and ruthless, and Ahab was relatively civilised and reasonable.

Elijah never really recovered from Jezebel's death threat: *'May the gods deal with me, be it ever so severely, if by this time tomorrow I do not make your life like that of one of them.'*

This is the trigger that resulted in permanent panic. On the surface, it doesn't seem like much. Elijah had faced death threats before. What made this so different? The seemingly innocuous phrase, *'the gods',* may well veil a vengeful summoning of the 69 brothers of Baal.

'Try this for size,' Jezebel basically said to Elijah. 'Your God might be able to defeat Baal but are you ready to fight the armies of his entire family? Is your God capable of taking on every single principality, all of the guardian-gods of the nations, in one go? Can your God fight a war on that many fronts?'

Elijah eventually discovered the answer to these questions. It took him about seven hundred years, but he finally realised it was indeed possible to face all the principalities at once. In fact, it was possible to walk straight into their war council and confront them. He was there when it happened. So too was John the apostle.

> *After six days Jesus took with Him Peter, James and John… and led them up a high mountain by themselves. There He was transfigured before them. His face shone like the sun, and His clothes became as white as the light. Just then there appeared before them Moses and Elijah, talking with Jesus.*
>
> *Peter said to Jesus, 'Lord, it is good for us to be here. If you wish, I will put up three shelters—one for You, one for Moses and one for Elijah.'*
>
> *While he was still speaking, a bright cloud covered them, and a voice from the cloud said, 'This is My Son, whom I love; with Him I am well pleased. Listen to Him!'*

When the disciples heard this, they fell facedown to the ground, terrified.

Matthew 17:1-6^{NIV}

Now nothing here designates the scene as a war council, until we realise this is the fulfillment of Psalm 82.

God has taken His place in the divine council;
in the midst of[108] *the gods He holds judgment:*
'How long will you judge unjustly and show partiality to the wicked?

Selah

Give justice to the weak and the orphan;
maintain the right of the lowly and the destitute.
Rescue the weak and the needy; deliver them from the hand of the wicked.'
They have neither knowledge nor understanding,
they walk around in darkness; all the foundations of the earth are shaken.
I say, 'You are gods, children of the Most High, all of you;
nevertheless, you shall die like mortals, and fall like any prince.'
Rise up, O God, judge the earth;
for all the nations belong to You!

Psalm 82^{NRS}

The high mountain above Caesarea Philippi was where the 'young lions', the brothers of Baal, met in assembly. Jesus stood up in the council of the very same principalities Jezebel had called on—and the voice of God had proclaimed their rule and reign to be over.

God changed the government. Elijah had failed to do it but Jesus did not. Shortly after coming down the mountain, Jesus divided

---

[108] 'In the midst of' is identical to one of the Hebrew words for *war*.

His disciples into pairs and sent seventy of them out to the villages of Galilee and Samaria.

Yes, Galilee of the Gentiles and Samaria the despised. The same nation where Elijah was supposed to divide up 7000 people who had not bowed the knee to Baal and send them out under the direction of 100 prophets to proclaim and restore the true government of Yahweh. There would have been bands of 70, exactly the same size as the band Jesus sent out. Jesus never said Elijah had failed but His actions speak loudly. He, not the Baptiser, completed the work of Elijah—He changed the world by turning the hearts of the children to the fathers and the hearts of the fathers to their children.

7.4 Love, Love, Love

> *So when they had eaten breakfast, Jesus said to Simon Peter, 'Simon, son of Jonah, do you **LOVE** Me more than these?'*
>
> *He said to Him, 'Yes, Lord; You know that I **love** You.'*
>
> *He said to him, 'Feed My lambs.'*
>
> *He said to him again a second time, 'Simon, son of Jonah, do you **LOVE** Me?'*
>
> *He said to Him, 'Yes, Lord; You know that I **love** You.'*
>
> *He said to him, 'Tend My sheep.'*
>
> *He said to him the third time, 'Simon, son of Jonah, do you **love** Me?' Peter was grieved because He said to him the third time, 'Do you **love** Me?'*
>
> *And he said to Him, 'Lord, You know all things; You know that I **love** You.'*
>
> *Jesus said to him, 'Feed My sheep.'*
>
> John 21:15–17^{NKJV}

It's well-known that Jesus twice used the word 'agápē' for *love*[109] in this interchange and, for the third question, used 'philía',

---

109 Emphasised in bold italics.

affection for a friend.¹¹⁰ Simon Peter, on the other hand, responded each time with 'philía'.

'Love' is a catch-all word in English. It is undifferentiated, although it has many nuances and shades, ranging across a spectrum from intense emotion to mere preference.

Greek, on the other hand, is known for distinguishing *at least* seven words for our one:

- storgē, *maternal* or *familial love*
- érōs, *erotic* or *sexual love*
- ludus, *playful affection*
- philía, *friendship*
- philautia, *self-love*
- pragma, *enduring love*
- agápē, *self-sacrificial love*

This list isn't comprehensive. It doesn't include words like 'mania', *obsessive love*, or 'meraki', *creative passion*. So, held up against this menu of possibilities, the slogan 'Love is love' is so vague as to be meaningless.

In addition, none of the options in the list cover English expressions like: 'I love chocolate' or 'I love weekends' or 'I love the sea.'

Now not all of these Greek words are used in the gospels and epistles. Those that are found in the text were made famous by CS Lewis in his book, *The Four Loves*. They are: 'storgē', 'érōs', 'philía' and 'agápē'.

In English-speaking cultures, we tend to slide so fuzzily in our thinking between all sorts of so-called loves—which, in reality, range from simple liking to outright idolising—that we're all

---

110 Emphasised in bold.

too apt to categorise many of them wrongly. And quite possibly, the Greeks were just as sloppy about the way they used words for 'love' and weren't exactly sticklers when it came to precise technical meanings.

Ian Paul points out the unexpected choices in John's gospel: 'people loved (*agape*-love) the darkness rather than light in John 3:19 and that the Pharisees loved (*agape*-love) the approval of men more than the praise of God in John 12:43. On the other hand, John uses *phileo* (in various forms)... and this includes the Father loving (*phileo*-love) the Son in John 5:20, Lazarus, whom Jesus loved (*phileo*-love) in John 11:13 and 11:36, Barrett's example of God's love in John 16.27, and the disciple whom Jesus loved (*phileo*-love) in John 20:2.'[111]

It's quite possible Jesus moderated His words to Simon Peter down from agápē, *sacrificial love*, to phileo, *friendship*—but it's also possible the words were being used interchangeably. Simon's distress centred around being asked three times. The repetition would have been disturbing enough in its own right but, by the third question, he was sure to have been reminded of his triple denial by the fireside in Caiaphas' courtyard.

Simon, when Jesus met him by the lake, had just turned his back on being Cephas, *rock*, the cornerstone whose statement of faith was the foundation of the church. That name, Cephas, has—yet again—governmental overtones. It's basically the same name as that of the High Priest, Caiaphas. And it tells us what the calling of Caiaphas was—his destiny was to be the first to proclaim the Messiah. That's the purpose for which God had called him to the office of High Priest. But he had turned away from the governmental mandate God had appointed him to accomplish.

---

111 psephizo.com/biblical-studies/are-there-different-loves-in-john-21/ (accessed 19 November 2021)

Jesus, in re-naming Simon as 'Cephas', appointed him to take the place Caiaphas should have assumed. Simon was given the mantle of government leader—to advance the Kingdom of Heaven and mandate its policies of love, joy, peace, patience, kindness, goodness, faithfulness, gentleness and self-control throughout the world.

Elijah had been given a governmental task, and twice he had failed to implement it. Caiaphas had been given a governmental task and he too had failed to implement it. Simon Peter was on the edge of the cliff. He'd lost his faith—if there was any left, it was hanging by a thread. He'd betrayed his Rabbi. He'd cast off his calling.

But Jesus, interestingly, doesn't talk about faith or belief, as He'd recently done with Thomas. He didn't raise the question of loyalty or honesty or failure to maintain integrity. He very simply talked love, love, love.

7.5 Identity and Identification

> *I will give to each one a white stone, and on the stone will be engraved a new name that no one understands except the one who receives it.*
>
> Revelation 2:17^{NLT}

THE FIRST GIFT GOD GAVE TO ADAM—after the gifts of life and work—was the right and privilege of naming the animals. The first *'new'* gift God bestows on believers, as detailed in the vision recorded in Revelation is a name on a white stone.

Names and naming herald the beginning of creation. God, as already mentioned, used His own name as the active creative principle to bring light into being. And, according to some rabbis, He also used naming in His creation of mankind:

> *And Jehovah God formed man of the dust of the ground, and breathed into his nostrils the breath* [Hebrew: nashamah] *of life; and man became a living soul.*
>
> Genesis 2:7^{ASV}

Because the word for *breath*, 'nashamah', contains the element 'shem', meaning *name*, it is considered that, whenever God creates a soul, He whispers a name to us. He calls us by name. He calls the stars by name.

> *Look up and see! Who created these? He brings out the stars by number; He calls all of them by name.*
>
> Isaiah 40:26 CSB

> *He calls his own sheep by name and leads them out.*
>
> John 10:3 NIV

God gifted to mankind the regency of names with all of their creative impulse and generative power. It was one of the tragic losses of the fall—that names too became one of the treasures the satan wants to accumulate for his own realm.

> *When the day came for the heavenly beings to appear before the Lord, Satan was there among them. The Lord asked him, 'What have you been doing?'*
>
> *Satan answered, 'I have been walking here and there, roaming around the earth.'*
>
> Job 1:6–7 GNT

The Hebrew word in this instance, 'shuwt', *walking here and there*, is also a word for *despise, hold in contempt, scourging, whipping, swerving* and *rowing a ship*.[112] There is another word for *walking here and there* or *going to and fro* used three times in the description of the satan's activities in Ezekiel 28. There it is usually translated *trading* but has overtones of *slander*. There is a deep sense in which this word, 'rekullah', means *trading in names*, and therefore trafficking in identities, destinies, vocations and callings.

It is no wonder that John, within the opening and closing sections of his gospel, has such a strong emphasis on identity. The reclaiming of names and titles from the enemies of God is one of

---

[112] No doubt this last meaning was because the rowers on a ship were whipped to keep them working.

his key themes—soon to become explicit in the 'I Am' statements of Jesus.

He heralds this intention with the three 'who are you?' questions posed to the Baptiser. That is the start of a thread that continues on scene after scene through the identification of the Lamb of God, the designation of the Messiah and the recognition of the King of Israel.

7.6 The Voice

'I am a voice of one calling in the wilderness, "Make straight the way for the Lord."'

John 1:23^{BSB}

Amongst the Hebrew teachers of ancient times, a distinctive mode of education was most highly favoured. The rabbi would frame a question or make a statement involving a particular Scriptural reference and the student would be expected to respond with a comment on the next verse or the following passage. Context was paramount—that was the main lesson.

When God turned up in a whirlwind and asked that magisterial set of questions at the end of the Book of Job, it's not—as so many people think—that He was slapping Job down and making sure he knew his rightful place. God was actually returning many of the questions Job had already put to Him earlier and adding in more information. This is a revelation of the Divine Rabbi expanding the mind of one of His favourite students, not some supercilious Superior slamming a pesky pupil back into line. The very difficulty of the questions bespeaks high honour.

So, when the Baptiser identified himself as the Voice in the wilderness, he would have expected his listeners to know the lines that followed:

> *'Every valley shall be exalted, and every mountain and hill shall be made low. The uneven shall be made level, and the*

> rough places a plain. The glory of Yahweh shall be revealed, and all flesh shall see it together; for the mouth of Yahweh has spoken it.'
>
> The voice of one saying, 'Cry!'
>
> One said, 'What shall I cry?'
>
> 'All flesh is like grass, and all its glory is like the flower of the field. The grass withers, the flower fades, because Yahweh's breath blows on it. Surely the people are like grass. The grass withers, the flower fades; but the word of our God stands forever.'...
>
> Lift up your voice with strength. Lift it up. Don't be afraid. Say to the cities of Judah, 'Behold, your God!'...
>
> He will feed His flock like a shepherd. He will gather the lambs in His arm, and carry them in His bosom. He will gently lead those who have their young.
>
> Isaiah 40:4–11 ^{WEB}

Even though the Baptiser had just denied being the Elijah-who-was-to-come, he still claimed a small portion of that herald's role. Those who heard and understood the message would have realised that the Baptiser was the Voice who was getting ready to say, *'Behold your God!'* And the way this would be indicated was through a proclamation involving sheep, lambs, or a shepherd.

John was priming his disciples for a momentous announcement. And there were those among them who did indeed understand what he was saying. Just two, apparently. But two was enough.

Especially when Andrew of Bethsaida, Simon Peter's brother, was one of them. From the very moment we are introduced to him, we discover his unique talent: he was the disciple who, more than any other, constantly brought people to Jesus.

Now the Pharisees who had been sent
questioned Him, 'Why then
do you baptise if you are not
the Messiah, nor Elijah,
nor the Prophet?'

'I baptise with water,'
John replied, 'but among you
stands One you do not know.
He is the one who comes after me, the
straps of whose sandals
I am not worthy to untie.'

This all happened at Bethany
on the other side of the Jordan, where John
was baptising.

John 1:24-28

He said, 'Throw your net on the right side of the boat and you will find some.' When they did, they were unable to haul the net in because of the large number of fish...

Simon Peter climbed back into the boat and dragged the net ashore. It was full of large fish, 153, but even with so many the net was not torn. Jesus said to them, 'Come and have breakfast.'

None of the disciples dared ask Him, 'Who are You?' They knew it was the Lord. Jesus came, took the bread and gave it to them, and did the same with the fish. This was now the third time Jesus appeared to His disciples after He was raised from the dead.

John 21:6, 11, 19

8.1 Side, Sandals and Fish

I must admit I hesitated even to try to match these sections. I couldn't see any immediate connection between sandals and fish and so decided, rather too quickly as it turned out, that it was expecting far too much for John to have mirror-linked all the finer details. Broad brushstrokes, yes, of course—but not the sort of high precision that would mean I'd have to solve the riddle of why a sandal was like a fish. I was quite satisfied with this rationalisation until I happened to open a box of chocolate fish.

It was the 153rd anniversary of our church and, as part of the celebrations, we planned to hand out some chocolate fish. It took a while to get them, because they are a confectionary item from New Zealand. As I looked at the wrapper, I noticed something unusual. There were a pair of thongs—that is, jandals, flip-flops, slops, zories, chappal, clam-diggers, chinelo, tsinelas or whatever other local name flat rubber footwear might be known by—and they were shaped like fish.

I stared at it far too long, wondering if my eyes were deceiving me. Then I decided it was a sign. That God was saying to me I'd been too hasty in dismissing any connection between fish and sandals. So, with that thought in mind, I went back to the text and scrutinised it much more intently.

Observant Jews respect Yom Kippur, the Day of Atonement, by practising 'affliction'. For many centuries, one custom involving 'affliction' was the prohibition of 'ne'ilat ha-sandal', *enclosing of the feet*.[113] Today this tradition is honoured more in the breach than in the observance. It is not known whether the practice dates back as far as the first century—however, the fact John the Baptiser mentions sandals on Yom Kippur strongly suggests it was already part of popular custom.

In a subtle reprimand, the Baptiser seems to have chided the messengers from Jerusalem for their casual attitude. Yom Kippur was not a day to be insistently quizzing anyone about their identity or their mission. If there was any day in the year reserved for repentance and affliction of soul, this was it.

It was set apart: 'holy'.

God had declared in instituting it:

> *'It is a Sabbath of solemn rest to you, and you shall afflict yourselves; it is a statute forever.'*
>
> Leviticus 16:31[ESV]

It was as if John was saying: 'Show some respect. For the Day, if not for me.' His implication: take off your sandals...

> *... for you stand on holy ground.*

That had been a command to Moses at Sinai, and Joshua at Gilgal.

The priests who ministered in the Temple went barefoot.[114] Paul's description of the Armour of God suggests a warrior-priest, since

---

113 etzion.org.il/en/talmud/seder-moed/massekhet-yoma/wearing-shoes-yom-kippur (accessed 28 November 2021)

114 See the Talmud, Yerushalmi Shekalim 5:1, fol. 48d, which, while its testimony is later than the first century, suggests this was always the case.

the 'shoes' he mentions are cloth strips. In English, we are given the impression of a legionnaire's sturdy hob-nailed boots, but the Greek is simply *underbindings*.

Who goes to war in socks?

Joshua—for one.

> When Joshua was near Jericho, he looked up and saw a man standing in front of him with a drawn sword in His hand. Joshua approached Him and asked, 'Are You for us or for our enemies?'
>
> 'Neither,' He replied. 'I have now come as Commander of the Lord's army.'
>
> Then Joshua bowed with his face to the ground in worship and asked Him, 'What does my Lord want to say to His servant?'
>
> The commander of the Lord's army said to Joshua, 'Remove the sandals from your feet, for the place where you are standing is holy.' And Joshua did so.
>
> Joshua 5:13–15^{HCSB}

This happened at Gilgal, near Jericho, where the people renewed their covenant through circumcision. For fourteen years—through the battles against thirty-one kings and then through the period of surveying and distributing the land—this was the tribal encampment far behind the front lines. Recent archaeological evidence suggests it had a wide stone wall for a boundary and

was shaped like a sandal.¹¹⁵ There are many such structures to be found in the Jordan Valley that have been given the name *gilgalim* or *sandalim*—because their shape has been thought to be influenced by the words of God to Joshua:

> *I have given you every place on which the sole of your foot treads, just as I promised to Moses.*
>
> Joshua 1:3^{AMP}

Thus, the sandal symbolised *possession of land* or *inheritance*.

At this point, I am constrained to overcome my reluctance about gematria because there's something very interesting hidden in the numeric values of God's promise to Joshua. The literal Hebrew for this verse is: 'Every place that the sole of your foot will tread upon, to you have I given, as I promised Moses.'

Now the numeric value of the following words, *'Every place that the sole of your foot will tread upon'*, happens to be 1734 or 17 × 17 × 6. But if we include *'have I given'*, the total becomes 2600. Adding in 1 for the 'kollel',¹¹⁶ we obtain 2601 which is 17 × 153.

---

115 The word *sandal* is not, however, first century Hebrew. It entered the language at a later date. It is a Greek word and appears to have originally meant the shoe of the Lydian god *Sandal* or Sandon. The Lydians believed their royal house descended from him and their capital Sardis may have been named after him. He was conflated with Heracles. 'In honour of Sandan-Heracles there was celebrated every year in Tarsus a funeral pyre festival, at the climax of which the image of the god was burned. The dying of nature under the withering heat of the summer sun and its resurrection to new life was the content of this mystery, which at once suggests its kinship with the cults of the Syrian Adonis, the Phrygian Attis, the Egyptian Osiris, and the Babylonian Tammuz.' The pyre of Sandan is featured on coins of Tarsus. Lions are also associated with him. (balashon.com/2007/09/sandal.html, accessed 29 June 2021)

116 The addition of a *kollel* is not simply for the word itself but for the silence within the word. See: David Patterson, *Wrestling with the Angel: Towards a Jewish Understanding of the Nazi Assault on the Name*, Paragon House 2006

This hints at an explanation to the mystery of the 153 fish in the matching chiastic passage. It's about inheritance. In the first chapter of Deuteronomy, Moses reports that God said:

> *Joshua the son of Nun, who stands before you, he shall go in there. Encourage him, for he shall cause Israel to inherit it.*
>
> Deuteronomy 1:38[NKJV]

The words *'he shall cause to inherit'* are one of a handful of Hebrew phrases with a gematria of 153. Again, the reference is to Joshua and inheritance. Through a subtle reference to sandals, John the apostle in his writing echoed this understanding of 153 with reference to the new Joshua: Jesus of Nazareth. By the end of the gospel, the 'territory' that Jesus won would have been obvious to any first century reader through the 'signs' He displayed.

This territory marked by sandals reflects the ancient tradition of placing rocks on top of used footwear to indicate the boundaries of a parcel of land and thereby delineate the extent of an inheritance. It was forbidden to move these sacred border markers for they specified the corners of the next generation's legacy. The heirs would inherit what was 'between the sandals'.

Now back in John's second-last chapter, there's a phrase with the same value—'the Magdalene'.[117] As will be shown in the next volume of this series, *The Summoning of Time*, she has a surprising connection to dispossession and a regaining of inheritance.

This is not the end of the references to 153. One Greek word of value 153 occurs in the breakfast-by-the-lake scene with Jesus. Is this simple coincidence? Hardly!

The word in question is *side*.

---

117 Mary is consistently called 'Miriam *the* Magdalene' in the fourth gospel.

8.2 The Sandal: Conquest and Romance

*'Throw your net on the right **side** of the boat...'*

John 21:6^{NIV}

The Greek word for *side*, 'meros', with its ever-so-appropriate gematria of 153, is not restricted to John 21. It occurs 41 other times throughout Scripture. However, this is the only instance where it is translated *side*. Elsewhere it is given as *share, portion, piece, part, country, region, district, division* or *section*. It is derived from 'meiromai', meaning *to be assigned an allotment, to be appointed a destiny, to receive by lot, to be given a portion that is due*.

Its deeper resonance is therefore *inheritance*. This is confirmed by its association in John's account with *net*. There are several Hebrew words for *net*, but one, 'resheth', has the distinction of being derived from 'yarash', *inheritance*. Jesus is not simply saying, *'Throw your net on the right side.'* Layered into those words is His call to His disciples: *'Align your inheritance with the destiny appointed for it.'*

For the Jewish people, inheritance implied the land and their destiny within it. Oftentimes they forgot their calling as a light to the nations, but this is the heritage that Jesus called them back to. Embedded in the story of the breakfast by the lake is a passing of authority, a transfer of a legacy, a commissioning—and the authority being conferred is tremendous. This was not simply about the handover of Elijah's mantle, but also about continuing the mission of Joshua. Yet this time the conquest is not only about prevailing in the Promised Land but looking forward to a victory that encompasses the entire world. It's about taking the message of redemption out to the ends of the earth.

Just as the word 'meros', *side*, is associated with *inheritance*, so too an untied sandal has the same connotation behind it.

Back in the first chapter, the matching section to this passage in the last chapter involves the Baptiser's comment:

> *'He is the one who comes after me, the straps of whose sandals I am not worthy to untie.'*
>
> John 1:27^{BSB}

As we've seen, this evokes Joshua and Moses on holy ground, as well as the priests in the Temple. Yet once we've also added in all the nuances of inheritance, it also evokes the untying of a sandal by the kinsman-redeemer in the story of Ruth and Boaz.

> *During Israel's earlier history, all things concerning redeeming or changing inheritances were confirmed by a man taking off his sandal and giving it to the other party, thereby creating a public record in Israel.*
>
> Ruth 4:7^{ISV}

This comment is made on the action of the kinsman-redeemer who gave up his right to inherit property because it also entailed marrying a widow. By taking off and handing over his sandal, he passed to Boaz the rights and privileges of the kinsman-redeemer. Perhaps the symbolism of the action was: 'Take this sandal as a legal confirmation that you can walk where I cannot.'

The story of Ruth and Boaz begins as a tale of an impoverished widow before changing its perspective to that of a bridegroom who recognises the presence of God in his field and looks for who is carrying it.[118]

John, in so subtly evoking the great romance of Scripture,[119] lays the groundwork for one of his primary themes: the coming of the Bridegroom of the world.

---

118 Chaim Bentorah says: 'In the story of Ruth, the words *YHWH imakem* are translated by practically all English translations as "The Lord be with you." The word "be" is not in the Hebrew text. We need a verb in English to complete a sentence but Hebrew does not need a verb to complete a sentence. Hence it is up to the translator to guess what the proper verb should be. This appears to be a greeting so we use the word "be." But the Jewish sages teach it is not a greeting. In fact grammatically it is not in a cohortative (expressing a desire or wish) form but is a statement of fact. "The Lord is with you." In other words, *the Lord is here*. When Boaz entered the field he felt the presence of the Lord.'

  facebook.com/ChaimBentorahMinistries/posts/4369475506498038 (accessed 1 December 2021)

119 See tarsusdarkstar.wordpress.com/2014/12/13/i-am-not-worthy-to-de-sandal-the-kinsman-redeemer-a-sermon-on-john-1-19-29/ (accessed 1 November 2021)

8.3 Immanuel, the Fish and the Logos

There's a famous story about Karl Friedrich Gauss, one of the most distinguished mathematicians of all time. His talent was evident from an early age. His teacher told the class to add up all the numbers from 1 to 100. Moments later, Gauss appeared at his desk with the correct answer: 5050. The boy later to be known as 'The Prince of Mathematicians' had figured out a short-cut. His cunning method of calculation actually works for all similar situations or for so-called 'triangular' numbers.[120] Triangular numbers have this name because, if they are arranged in rows of dots on paper, they form perfect triangles. However, they can also be found by adding successive whole numbers together. For instance, 171 is the eighteenth triangular number because all the numbers from 1 to 18 add to 171, while 153 is the seventeenth triangular number because all the numbers from 1 to 17 add to 153.

The first three 'perfect' numbers are also triangular numbers. 6 is the first perfect number and the third triangular number, 28 is the second perfect number and the seventh triangular number and

---

[120] The insight that Gauss had was this: in the sequence from 1 to 100, there are 50 pairs that add up to 101. They are 1 and 100, 2 and 99, 3 and 98, 4 and 97, 5 and 96, 6 and 95, 7 and 94 and so on. He multiplied 50 by 101 in his head—a kindergarten-simple calculation for those who know old-style times tables—and deduced the correct answer: 5050.

496 is the third perfect number and the 31st triangular number. So when John used 496 as the number of syllables in the prologue to his gospel and the number of words in the epilogue, he was using a number that was both perfect and triangular.

It wasn't a coincidence either. (Neither is the fact that my first paragraph in this section is 153 words and ends on the number 153, or that the first two paragraphs total 231 words.) John used two other triangular numbers in the sub-structure of 496. He used 171 and 325. And of course he mentioned 153 as the number of fish caught in the net when Jesus appeared to His disciples for the third time after His resurrection. Now, even though 496 is perfect and triangular, and also features in the prophecy of Immanuel, *God with us*, I really don't think God inspired John to highlight it so prominently for any of these reasons. I don't even think John used triangular numbers because he wanted to score a point against the Pythagoreans Gnostics amongst the Christians who believed numbers were gods—and triangular numbers the highest of all. I think his reason was mainly mathematical: a truly lovely geometrical theorem connects 496 to 153. When we multiply 496 by the golden ratio and divide by 2, we get 153.

Now remember the Greeks had a special name for the golden ratio: they called it the *logos*.

The gospel of John is therefore not just an exquisitely-told eyewitness story of various episodes in the life of Jesus, it is also a mathematical masterpiece as intricately designed as a sunflower or a hummingbird, a galaxy or a cell, a seashell or a fern-frond.

It links the Logos—as both Word and as corresponding Ratio—into the dynamics of the text, a text both fearfully and wonderfully made.

8.4 Archimedes and the 'Measure of the fish'

Archimedes of Syracuse was one of the most eminent mathematicians and inventors of ancient times, surpassing even Pythagoras in the extent of his fame. He was the original 'absent-minded professor'. The most widely known story about him tells of his discovery of a method for determining the volume of an object with an irregular shape.

King Hiero II had ordered a votive crown for a temple, and had supplied the craftsman with a quantity of pure gold. But, on delivery, he became suspicious that some silver had been substituted. So he asked Archimedes to determine the truth of the matter—without damaging the crown in the process.

It was a difficult scientific problem. Archimedes was getting into his bath, pondering it, when inspiration came to him. 'Eureka!' he yelled. 'I have it!' And, in his excitement, he jumped up and

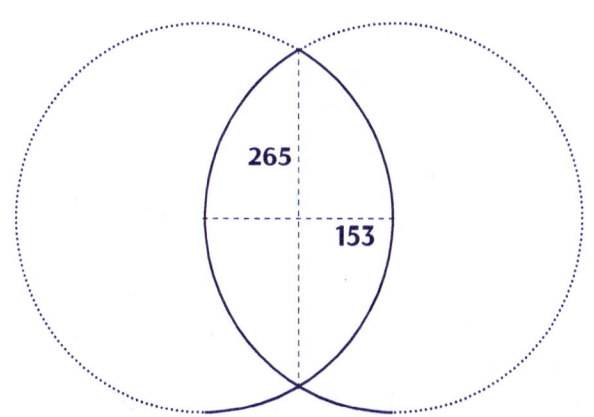

dashed out into the street, calling, 'Eureka!' and forgetting he'd left his clothes behind.[121]

Archimedes was also a geometer of renown. He'd apparently died during the siege of Syracuse, while trying to work out a theorem in the sand. He was so preoccupied with solving the problem he failed to get out of the way of an invading Roman soldier who cut him down, despite a general order to ensure his safety.[122]

One of the most well-known geometrical theorems solved by Archimedes was known as 'the measure of the fish'. When two circles overlap, so that the circumference of one touches the centre of the other, then a 'fish shape' is formed. This was called the 'Vesica

---

[121] Archimedes, whose name means *master planner* or *foremost counsellor*, was the most famous inventor of the ancient world. As a practical thinker rather than a philosophical one, he has been admired across the millennia. His renown in the first century was unsurpassed. In pondering the problem the king had set him, he realised that the level of the water in the tub rose as he got in, so this effect could be used to determine the volume of the crown. For practical purposes water is incompressible, so the submerged crown would displace an amount of water equal to its own volume. By dividing the mass of the crown by the volume of water displaced, the density of the crown could be obtained. This density would be lower than that of gold if cheaper and less dense metals had been added. The test on the crown was conducted successfully, proving that silver had indeed been mixed in. (en.wikipedia.org/wiki/Archimedes, accessed 1 December 2021) This test for the purity of metal was well-known in first century Judea amongst the money-changers. To pay the Temple tax, a shekel or half-shekel of the highest quality silver from the mint in Tyre was the only acceptable coinage. However unscrupulous dealers would melt down a coin, then use the silver as a thin plating on a lead base. They'd counterfeit many 'shekels' from the one. Fraudulent coins could be detected by using Archimedes' water test. The shekels carried an image of the Phoenician god of death, Hercules Melqart. And perhaps that was the subtle symbolic message Jesus was conveying to His disciples in using 153, a number so closely associated with Archimedes and water. Just as the water test for fraud devised by Archimedes was used to check the death-imprinted Temple shekels, so baptism and repentance, as death to self, reveal how genuine a disciple's allegiance to Him is.

[122] His last words were reputedly, 'Do not disturb my circles.'

Piscis' or *fish bladder*. It was also considered to be a lens, and was further known as a 'mandorla', an almond-shaped aureole.

In the Vesica Piscis, the ratio of the length of the fish to its width is always the same, regardless of the size of the circles. In modern notation, this ratio is $1/\sqrt{3}$. However in ancient Greece, square root symbolism had not been developed, so this number had to be approximated by the nearest ratio or fraction. The length compared to the width equalled 265: 153. This became known as 'the measure of the fish'.

So in having 153 *fish*, as compared to, say, 153 *sheep*, the actions of Jesus show a playful sense of humour as well as acute mathematical awareness. But is there something deeper here? Is there a hint of a stinging rebuke? If not to the disciples on the beach, then to the Gnostics with their mathematical obsessions?

Archimedes was in his bath when he received an inspiration—an 'in-spiriting' moment. John the Baptiser was shortly to testify that he was a witness to the 'in-spiriting' of Jesus at His baptism when the Holy Spirit descended from heaven in the form of a dove.

A bath is not a baptism. Inspiration is not about genius[123] in mathematics or science; it's about the Holy Spirit in-dwelling us, and the tabernacling of God in our midst.

A bath is about cleansing; baptism is about repentance.

---

123 From Latin *genius*, 'guardian deity or spirit which watches over each person from birth; spirit, incarnation; wit, talent'. (See etymonline.com, accessed 1 December 2021)

8.5 The Inheritors

In our times, the most common symbol of Christianity is the cross—whether it's on top of a church or on a chain around someone's neck. However in the first century when the sight of a Roman cross automatically brought 'crucifixion' and 'execution' to mind, it was hardly an appropriate motif.

Another common symbol today is the 'fish', sometimes with the Greek letters for 'ichthus' enclosed by the outline. Now 'ichthus' means *fish*, and it was used as an acronym for **I**ēsous **Ch**ristos **Th**eou **U**ios **S**oter, which is: Jesus (**I**) Christ (**CH**), God's (**TH**) Son (**U**), Saviour (**S**).

Jesus Himself was called a fish in a treatise by Tertullian who lived in the late second and early third century. Writing on baptism, *De Baptismo 1*, he says that as water sustains fish, 'we, little fishes, after the image of our *ichthus*, Jesus Christ, are born in the water (of baptism), nor are we safe but by remaining in it.'[124]

Because the shape of the *ichthus* was easy to draw in sand with a toe or the tip of a sandal, Christians used to trace it, apparently idly, in order to identity one another during times of persecution. It was a subtle way of testifying to faith without shouting it to the

---

[124] earlychurchhistory.org/christian-symbols/the-fish-symbol-ichthus/ (accessed 3 December 2021)

world. Besides the hidden inbuilt code of *Jesus Christ, God's Son, Saviour*, it was also a reminder of the calling of the first disciples to be 'fishers of men'.

In his surreal television series, *The Prisoner*, star and scriptwriter Patrick McGoohan used a variation on the fish as an identifying symbol for the underground resistance. 'Be seeing you,' someone would say while saluting from the eye with the thumb and forefinger held together. This gesture, at least to me, looks much more like the lens of an eye than a fish. McGoohan maintained the gesture went back to early Christianity, but I have yet to find a source for his claim. Yet I don't discount it entirely. It has a fair bit of an authentic 'feel' to it. And the reason I say that is because, not only does the gesture look like a lens, it also looks like an almond.

Watching—or *looking alert* and *being awake*—and almonds are curiously connected in Hebrew. The prophet Jeremiah reported:

> *Again the Lord spoke His word to me and asked, 'Jeremiah, what do you see?'*
> *I answered, 'I see a branch of an almond tree.'*
> *Then the Lord said to me, 'Right. I am watching to make sure that My words come true.'*
>
> Jeremiah 1:11–12^{GWT}

Now, this interchange doesn't make much sense in English. But in Hebrew, it's a question-and-answer that revolves around a pun—the word for *almond* sounds just like that for *watching*. And without the almond-like lens within the eye, no one can watch effectively.

While we're on the subject of puns, let's note that the first symbol of Christianity—which was not the fish, or the lens, or the almond, or the cross—was also based on a pun. The honour for the original symbol for the followers of The Way actually goes to the *anchor*.

> *We have this hope as an anchor for our lives.*
>
> Hebrews 6:19^{GNT}

The anchor symbol was used on the earliest tombs of Christian believers. The emblem was chosen because 'en kurio', *in the Lord*, sounded so much like 'ankura', *anchor*.

It was through symbolism that the inheritors of the kingdom of heaven identified one another. It so often still is. A cross on a necklace is, generally speaking, a statement of faith. It's a pity, really. After all, Jesus said:

> *By their fruit you will recognise them.*
>
> Matthew 7:20^{NIV}

and:

> *This is how everyone will know that you are My disciples, if you have love for one another.*
>
> John 13:35^{ISV}

John's epistle tells us that, being disciples of Christ, we are also part of God's family:

> *Beloved, we are now children of God, and what we will be has not yet been revealed. We know that when Christ appears, we will be like Him, for we will see Him as He is.*
>
> 1 John 3:2^{BSB}

The original household of God, in its garden setting on a mountain watered by four rivers, included both humanity and angelic beings traditionally called the 'Sons of God'. Some of these majestic spirits rebelled, came to earth, sought out beautiful women and then sired mighty and monstrous men with them. The flood in the time of Noah destroyed the giant offspring of this first influx of angels—the flood that, as Peter tells us, is the symbol of baptism:

> *So He went and preached to the spirits in prison—those who disobeyed God long ago when God waited patiently while Noah was building his boat. Only eight people were saved from drowning in that terrible flood. And that water is a picture of baptism, which now saves you, not by removing dirt from your body, but as a response to God from a clean conscience. It is effective because of the resurrection of Jesus Christ.*
>
> 1 Peter 3:19–21^{NLT}

Here we see revealed another reason, perhaps the major one, why John has linked and matched the two scenes—in the first chapter the baptism of repentance preached by the Baptiser and in the final chapter, the post-resurrection breakfast by the water. It's the resurrection that makes baptism effective. It is through the power of the cross and resurrection, rather than our own willpower, that repentance becomes an about-face that manifests the fruit of love and demonstrates our status as children of God.

The angelic *'sons of God'*—a phrase with a gematria[125] of 153—forfeited the inheritance of heaven for lust. The human children of God are called to take up that inheritance through love.

---

[125] intheword.blog/2020/03/27/153-sons-of-god/ (accessed 13 November 2021)

8.6 The Waters of Wadi Al-Yabis

The waters of baptism are a picture of the waters of the flood. So said Peter in his first epistle.

This symbolism was enhanced by the locality that John the Baptiser chose to begin his ministry. It was further complemented by the advent of the Holy Spirit.

The site is, in modern times, disputed. However, for many reasons, I believe that Bethany-beyond-the-Jordan should be correctly identified as the Wadi Al-Yabis in the presentday Hashemite Kingdom of Jordan. Not the least of these reasons is that this would mean that John the Baptiser began his ministry in the place anciently known as the Brook Cherith.

This would position him in exactly the same place as Elijah when he began his mission. The Brook Cherith was Elijah's hide-out at the start of the drought. It was the refuge where he was daily fed by ravens, a bird first mentioned towards the end of the flood story.

> At the end of forty days Noah opened the window of the ark that he had made and sent forth a raven. It went to and fro until the waters were dried up from the earth. Then he sent forth a dove from him, to see if the waters had subsided from the face of the ground. But the dove found no place to set her foot, and she returned to him to the ark, for the waters

were still on the face of the whole earth. So he put out his hand and took her and brought her into the ark with him. He waited another seven days, and again he sent forth the dove out of the ark. And the dove came back to him in the evening, and behold, in her mouth was a freshly plucked olive leaf. So Noah knew that the waters had subsided from the earth. Then he waited another seven days and sent forth the dove, and she did not return to him anymore.

Genesis 8:6–12^{ESV}

In the time of Elijah, the Brook Cherith was associated with ravens—birds reputed not even to feed their own young, but who yet provided food for the prophet. In the time of the Elijah-who-was-to-come, the place became associated with the descent of a dove.

Ravens feed on carrion—they are death-eaters. That is why the raven didn't need to return to Noah—it had floating provender wherever it flew. The dove, on the other hand, needed grain, seed, berries or greens—and until the trees reappeared and recovered sufficiently, it was dependent on Noah.

In the last winter of His life, Jesus retreated to Bethany-beyond-the-Jordan where He found refuge from those trying to kill Him. It was there that He received the news that Lazarus was ill. And it was there that He prepared to become the death-eater—the One who swallowed up Death and its sting. The raven-dove symbolism of this valley not only harks back to the flood but, in doing so, pictures its reversal. Instead of universal death, Jesus offers Himself to us as the Resurrection and the Life.

The Raven is emblematic of Jesus and the Dove of the Holy Spirit. Although we're used to the term 'Lamb' for Jesus and 'Dove' for the Spirit, it's surprising and somewhat disconcerting to encounter hidden images of the Lord as a Fish, a Raven and even—in relation to the mountain of spices brought to His tomb—a Stag.

Wadi Al-Yabis was a very significant place for the early Christians. Not far from it today are the ruins of the city of Pella, which attracts many tourists in spring when the hillsides are awash with spring flowers. When the Roman armies were marching to besiege Jerusalem, many believers fled to Pella, heeding the words of Jesus:

> *When you see 'the abomination that causes desolation' standing where it does not belong—let the reader understand—then let those who are in Judea flee to the mountains. Let no one on the housetop go down or enter the house to take anything out. Let no one in the field go back to get their cloak... Pray that this will not take place in winter.*
>
> Mark 13:14–18^{NIV}

Historians find the record of the 'flight to Pella' very doubtful—it makes no sense to them that the early Christians would elect to flee to such a bizarre place. Yet, the Wadi Al-Yabis is not a strange choice at all. Elijah chose to hide there, John the Baptiser started his ministry there[126] and even Jesus found refuge here.[127] If it's good enough for Jesus, John and Elijah, why wouldn't it be good enough for the faithful followers of the Lord?

---

126 This was before he moved to Aenon near Salim where the water was plentiful. Another reason for suggesting that Bethany-beyond-the-Jordan is situated in Wadi Al-Yabis is that Aenon was on the far bank, directly opposite the spot where the stream from this wadi flows into the Jordan River. It was conveniently in the same vicinity and therefore easy for pilgrims to find.

127 It's also possible that David had troops in this area when he was fleeing from Absalom. Mahanaim, the site of David's camp, is about 20 km south of Pella. The battle between David's forces and Absalom's took place in Gilead in the 'Forest of Ephraim'. Apparently this woodland lay between the Cherith and the Jabbok streams. Absalom was killed here.

8.7 *Is* **and** *Is Not*

> *None of them dared ask 'Who are You?'*
>
> John 21:12^{NIV}

IN HIS LAST CHAPTER, JOHN raises the question of identity—only to swiftly answer: *'They knew it was the Lord.'* And yet, the 'Who are You?' lingers as if, perhaps, while the response is correct, some essence of mystery remains.

Let us turn to the beginning to see if we can dispel just a little of the riddling aura here. In the parallel segment, the Baptiser is quizzed about his identity and his replies fall into categories of *is* and *is not*.

I am *not* Elijah.

I am *not* the Prophet sent from God who would be like Moses.

I am *not* the Christ.

I am *not* the 'goel', *the kinsman-redeemer.* As a matter of fact, I'm not even worthy to untie His sandal, even though His desire is to hand it over so we can inherit the land He walks on.

Later, he basically also says: I am *not* the Bridegroom. However he does admit to being a 'shoshbin', *Friend of the Bridegroom.*[128] And of course, he also admits to being the Herald's Voice.

Curiously he denied being the Elijah-who-is-to-come—yet Jesus affirmed this is indeed who he was.

> *I tell you no one ever born on this earth is greater than John the Baptist. But whoever is least in the kingdom of heaven is greater than John… And if you believe them, John is Elijah, the prophet you are waiting for.*
>
> Matthew 11:11–14[CEV]

It would be easy to simply dismiss the Baptiser as being mistaken in his humble view of himself and take Jesus' word for it. Yet I think it's more complicated than that. In a certain sense, they're both right. The Baptiser both *is* and *is not* the promised Elijah.

Practically speaking, Jesus fulfilled far more of the role of the Elijah-who-is-to-come than John the Baptiser did.

First and most definitely, the angel Gabriel declared:

> *'Many of the sons of Israel he will turn back to the Lord their God. And he will go on before the Lord in the spirit and power of Elijah, to turn the hearts of the fathers to their children and the disobedient to the wisdom of the righteous—to make ready a people prepared for the Lord.'*
>
> Luke 1:16–17[BSB]

---

128 John 3:29

Second, he dressed like Elijah—in a hairy garment with a leather belt. Third, he started his ministry at the Brook Cherith, just like Elijah, where an unusual visitation by birds occurred.[129] Fourth, both witnessed the heavens opening. Fifth, both concentrated their ministries in the region corresponding to the ancient Northern Kingdom. Sixth, both focused on calls for repentance. Seventh, both talked companionably with a king, even while confronting him. Eighth, in both cases, the king's palace was in Samaria. Ninth, both made implacable enemies of the king's wife.

In contrast, Jesus unquestionably lacked 'the look'. No camel hair tunic or leather belt. However He too started His ministry at the Brook Cherith. He too concentrated His ministry in Galilee, Samaria and the Decapolis—the region once ruled by the Northern Kingdom, centred in Samaria. He too called for repentance and His disciples baptised others, just as John's did. He too criticised Herod, calling him, *'that fox.'* (Luke 13:32[KJV]) There is no indication He made an enemy of Herod's wife. Yet in other ways He paralleled Elijah.

Elijah went out into the desert for forty days and was ministered to by an angel along the way. Jesus was driven out into the desert for forty days and was also ministered to by angels.

Elijah went to Zarephath, near Tyre and Sidon, and helped a widow and her son after asking for part of her last meal. Jesus likewise went to the region of Tyre and Sidon and there He helped a woman and her daughter after she demonstrated her faith by asking Him for the 'crumbs' of His ministry of healing.

---

129 Ravens sent by God came with meat for Elijah—unusual in that they are renowned for not even feeding their own young. John the Baptiser seems to have foraged for his own food of locust pods—carob—and wild honey. The unusual visitation in his time was Holy Spirit appearing as a dove, sent by God.

In addition, Jesus raised Lazarus from the dead—just as Elijah raised the son of the widow of Zarephath.[130] John the Baptiser did nothing of this kind.

So, yes, in many notable ways John fulfilled the role of Elijah, but it's undeniable that Jesus clocked up a few more. The grave of John the Baptiser is said to be in Sebaste in Samaria,[131] but there is no tomb for Elijah. He was caught up into the air, just as Jesus was at the ascension—although admittedly, Elijah's disappearance was much more dramatic. Yet the chariots of fire recall John's proclamation that Jesus would baptise in spirit and fire.

Moreover, Jesus also has aspects of Elisha, the servant of Elijah. When Jesus went to Nain, He raised to life a boy who was the only son of his widowed mother. Nain was close to the long-vanished town of Shunem—which, in its time, was a place often visited by Elisha. A woman of Shunem who supported Elisha's ministry had an only son who died. The prophet raised him from the dead in

---

130 The only person Elijah raised from the dead was this widow's son. His successor, Elisha, raised two people from the dead, in keeping with the double anointing he asked for: one was the son of the woman of Shunem and the other was a Moabite man who was hurriedly placed in Elisha's tomb when a band of raiders appeared. On touching Elisha's bones, he came alive. Jesus obviously plays with this idea of double anointing: He raised the son of the widow of Nain, Jairus' daughter and Lazarus. If we can count His own resurrection, it's four—double Elisha's double of Elijah. Then, of course, the raising becomes exponential with all the people who rose up from their graves after His resurrection (Matthew 27:53).

131 From about the fourth century, the grave of John was said to be at Sebaste in Samaria, next to the tombs of Elisha and Obadiah. How his bones came to be there is unknown. According to the historian Flavius Josephus, John had been beheaded in the fortress of Machaerus, in the Transjordan. In the time of Elijah, this region was also under the control of the king of Samaria. It is possible that, because John had many disciples in Samaria, they may have brought the body from Machaerus to Sebaste. On the other hand, local tradition, both Christian and Muslim, claims that the tomb of his parents Elizabeth and Zacharias is nearby and that he was simply brought 'home'.

the same vicinity that, eight centuries later, Jesus would do a very similar thing.

Why is it that Jesus is the Elijah-who-is-to-come just as much as John the Baptiser was? I believe it's because Jesus is the Author *and* Finisher of our faith. As the Finisher, He completes our calling: He puts the finishing touches to those divinely appointed tasks that we fail to fully realise, He accomplishes the work we start but do not bring to perfect fruition.

He is the kingly messiah, the war messiah, the priestly messiah, *and* the One who perfectly discharged the calling of the Elijah-who-is-to-come. All in one. He is fulfillment of both Elijah and John the Baptiser. And He is also the one who finishes the work of many, many more heroes of the faith.

'It is finished,' Jesus said on the cross. It's all too easy to overlook that the consummation of the work of salvation is also a completion of His vocation—and ours as well.

8.8 The Crushed Head and the Bruised Heel

'All is number' or 'God is number' was the dictum of the Brotherhood founded by Pythagoras of Samos. He was named for Python Apollo, the tutelary deity at the shrine of Delphi across the bay from the city of Corinth.

The shrine was famous for its sibyl, a priestess who delivered oracles in riddling, ambiguous statements or the babbling cadences of another language. Holding laurel leaves and a dish of spring water into which she gazed, the Pythia sat on a bronze tripod. This stool was positioned above a shaft into the earth to catch rising gases and situated near the omphalos, *the navel of the earth*, which was flanked by two solid gold eagles, representing the emissaries of Zeus who had been sent from opposite ends of the earth to locate its navel and had met in the skies above Delphi.[132]

It was here that Apollo had, according to legend, defeated the titanic serpent, Python, and thus acquired the title Python Apollo. The previous name of Delphi was Pytho, from the Greek word for *rot* and named for the sickly sweet smell of the decomposing monster.[133]

---

132 Zeus apparently wanted to locate the centre of the earth. So, according to legend, he sent two eagles from the ends of the world. Launched at the same moment and travelling at the same speed, they met at Delphi. Zeus, wanting a more precise GPS coordinate, threw a stone from the sky and where it fell was considered the omphalos, the navel of the earth. The heaven-sent stone itself was the navelstone—the Greek rival to the Hebrew 'eben ha-shetiyah', *the foundation stone of the universe*.

133 The original name was Krisa.

Over the centuries, the fame and wealth of Delphi became enormous. In the sixth century BC, Croesus, the immensely rich king of Lydia, sent to the Pythia to inquire whether he should mount a campaign against the Persians. Her reply, 'If Croesus invades, a great empire will be destroyed,' contained an ambiguity he failed to notice. The armies of Cyrus of Persia defeated Croesus about five years before they were victorious over Babylon.

This was the time when both Pythagoras and the prophet Daniel lived. At the time Daniel was in Babylon, Pythagoras was studying in Egypt. It was five years before the Persian armies swept down to Egypt and captured Pythagoras, carrying him off to Babylon. By that point, Daniel had been taken east to Susa and Ecbatana. They missed meeting each other by just a few years.

And there is no doubt they would have met, had Daniel remained in Babylon. Daniel was twice appointed chief of the magi while he was there, and Pythagoras studied with the magi—in fact, the famous theorem which bears his name is almost certainly not his own discovery but simply a part of the magi's routine knowledge of quadratic equations.

After Pythagoras was released and returned to Greece, before settling in Italy, he founded his Brotherhood—a fellowship that was devoted to the secrets of mathematics—quadratics in particular; to numbers as divinities; to vegetarianism; to a belief in reincarnation; and to the view that what is female is evil and untrustworthy.

The opening and closing few scenes of John's gospel roundly attack all these ideals: they focus on quadratic concepts in mathematics; they connect numbers to God but do not classify any as equal to the Godhead; they show the disciples and Jesus sharing fish and bread, not refraining from meat; they speak of resurrection not reincarnation; and they highlight the interaction of Jesus with two different women named Mary—implicitly accepting the Magdalene's testimony as trustworthy and true.

The infiltration of misogyny in the church has far more to do with Gnosticism than it does with any so-called Hebrew patriarchy. Right from the start, Jesus and His apostles were at war with the hatred of women that was associated with Greek culture and the Pythagorean cult in particular.

Women were a particular target of the serpent, ever since God spoke to the serpent in Eden, saying:

> *'I will put enmity between you and the woman, and between your seed and her seed. He will crush your head, and you will strike his heel.'*
>
> Genesis 3:15^{BSB}

The word *'heel'* in Hebrew is also the word, *'if'*—the signifier of choice. God granted the serpent the right to strike at the choices of humanity, to test them. When Jesus faced the devil in the wilderness, every test involved the word 'if' and a profound, far-reaching choice.

The word 'if' was indelibly associated with the worship of Python Apollo.

Before Nero became emperor, he visited the shrine at Delphi and asked about the curious symbol found throughout the complex—a stylised E engraved in gold, silver and wood. Plutarch, who was later to become the high priest at Delphi, wrote about Nero's visit and his question. No definitive answer could be given—the symbol was so ancient, its original meaning had been lost in the mists of time. However, Plutarch ventured seven possibilities:

(1) It was dedicated by the 'Wise Men', as a protest against interlopers, to show that their number was actually five and not seven (ei = e, the fifth letter, five).

(2) e is the second vowel, the Sun is the second planet, and Apollo is identified with the sun (ei = E, the second vowel).

(3) e means 'if': people ask the oracle IF they will succeed, or IF they should do this or that (ei = 'if').

(4) ei is used in wishes or prayers to the god, often in the combination εἴθε or εἰ γάρ (ei = 'if' or 'if only').

(5) ei, 'if,' is an indispensable word in logic for the construction of a syllogism (ei = 'if').

(6) Five is a most important number in mathematics, physiology, philosophy, and music (ei = e, 'five').

(7) ei means 'thou art' and is the address of the consultant to Apollo, to indicate that the god has eternal being (ei = 'thou art').[134]

In summary, Plutarch three times suggests that *e* refers to *if*, twice that it points to *five* and twice that it signifies *Apollo*. The final claim he put forward for Apollo is in direct opposition to Yahweh: Apollo is called the 'eternal being', or the 'everliving one'. He is to be honoured as 'thou art', and if we turn this mode of address around to consider how Apollo would speak of this title for himself, it would be 'I Am'.

This is a direct assault on the name of God. In addition, the image of the solid gold eagles flanking the omphalos, *the navelstone of the earth*, counterfeit the solid gold cherubim overshadowing the mercy seat while the omphalos mimics the 'eben ha-shetiyah', the earthly representation of the foundation stone of the cosmos.

It is inconceivable that John, if he knew about the claims of Python Apollo as the I Am, and as the arbiter of *if* and the choices associated with it, would not counter them in the strongest possible way. We miss the vehemence and the passion of his response to Pythagoreanism because we don't comprehend the import of the numbers he was using.

---

[134] loebclassics.com/view/plutarch-moralia_e_delphi/1936/pb_LCL306.195.xml (accessed 7 December 2021)

When he opened his gospel with a proclamation of the Logos, he set out to crush the head of Python by striking at Pythagoreanism. He made absolutely sure that anyone reading his message who was influenced by the religious views of the Brotherhood—either through Platonism or Gnosticism—didn't mistake Jesus, God made manifest, for the tetrakys or for the reincarnation of Pythagoras. John did this by simply making his opening sentence 17 words long. Today we're unlikely to notice this use of 17 and, even if we do, we're apt to shrug in complete indifference to it. However, any first century Greek reader knew that 17 was the 'atrocity' to be avoided at all costs.

In the philosophy of truth and beauty that dominated Greek art, architecture and literature, 17 was the 'antiphraxis', the *obstruction* that was viewed by the Pythagoreans with loathing and revulsion.[135] To the Greek readers of John's gospel, his opening line would have been an iconoclastic explosion: to unite the despised 17 with the exquisitely beautiful number, the *logos*, was unthinkable. To then end with 153 was to confirm that the eruption in the opening verse was not an accidental mistake of an ignorant barbarian but deliberate in intent.

---

135 Plutarch, the same high priest of Python Apollo who wrote *On the E at Delphi*, revealed this in an essay about Isis and Osiris. Much of what we know about the place of Isis and Osiris in Egyptian religion comes from Plutarch—which, for a modern parallel, is about the same as relying on the Dalai Lama for the secrets of the Sikh faith.

8.9 The Name of God

In Biblical times, names were considered to be an expression of both identity and destiny. The name Jesus is the English version of the Greek Iēsous, which corresponds to the Hebrew Yeshua,[136] *God saves*. This is an alternative for Yehoshua, or Joshua, with its opening syllable derived from 'yah', referring to Yahweh, traditionally used throughout Scripture as the name for God.

You may have noticed my careful phrasing of that last sentence: *traditionally used* throughout Scripture as the name for God. 'Yahweh' or YHWH, as it is in Hebrew, was allegedly the sacred name—the Tetragrammaton—too holy to be spoken. Actually, the name 'Yahweh' is a concealment device for the true sacred name. When God spoke to Moses at Mount Sinai, He did not reveal His name as Yahweh, *He is who He is*. He told Moses that His name is *I Am who I Am*.

---

136 Or Y'shua.

It's very cunning to change the way people spoke of God in this way. It solved two problems:

(1) Misuse of the sacred name in a profane way—either accidentally or deliberately.
(2) Revelation of the sacred name to foreign unbelievers.

In the ancient world, where aggressive nations actively sought the secret names of local deities in order to entice them to give up their defence of particular territory,[137] it would take someone with exceptional knowledge of the Hebrew language as well as an in-depth acquaintance with the Book of Exodus to figure out that 'Yahweh' was a grammatical step removed from the genuine name of the Most High. The name of Israel's God looked like it was out in the open, which was a measure of protection in itself. Even if any spies were suspicious enough to think it was far too easy to discover, it would be impossible to dig deeper without giving their hidden intentions away.

---

137 The Romans were notorious for searching out the secret names of the guardian gods of territories with which they were at war. Using a technique known as *elicio*, they would then invite the gods to Rome. If you knew the name of a god or goddess, you had power over that deity. The historian Livy describes how Camillus, ruler of Rome in around 396 BC broke the siege of the Etruscan city of Veii with this prayer and *elicio*: 'Guided and inspired by your will, Pythian Apollo, I go forth to destroy the city of Veii. To you I devote a tenth part of the spoils. And to you, Queen Juno, now dwelling in Veii, I beseech you to follow us after our victory to our City, which will become your city. There we will build you a temple worthy of your sublime majesty.'

At the time of Alexander the Great, the people of Tyre became concerned for their colossal statue of Apollo and so fastened it with gold chains so Alexander could not succeed in enticing it away. Images of Ares—the Greek equivalent of the Roman war god, Mars—were secured with magical bindings in several places of Asia Minor to ensure his protection did not suddenly disappear. Josephus, the Jewish historian, mentions the practice of *elicio*, carried out at the instigation of King Alexander Jannaeus, one of the Maccabees, who summoned a god of Edom to Jerusalem. Names are power. The whole of the ancient world knew it. (See Anne Hamilton, *God's Pageantry: The Threshold Guardians & the Covenant Defender*, Armour Books 2015)

Speaking from the burning bush,

> God said to Moses, 'I Am Who I Am'; and He said, 'You shall say this to the Israelites, "I AM has sent me to you."'
>
> Exodus 3:14^{AMP}

'I Am Who I Am' is 'Ehyeh asher Ehyeh', *not* 'Yahweh asher Yahweh'. I Am is 'Ehyeh', while 'Yahweh' is He Is.

The name God revealed to Abraham was El Shaddai, and the name He revealed to Moses was Ehyeh. The numerical value of Yahweh is 26. It will probably not be a surprise at this point that the gematria of aahweh, the archaic form of Ehyeh, is 17.[138]

Seven famous I Am statements appear in John's gospel: 'I am the Bread of Life', 'I am the Light of the World', 'I am the Good Shepherd', 'I am the Gate of the Sheep', 'I am the Resurrection and the Life', 'I am the True Vine', 'I am the Way, the Truth and the Life'. However, other 'I Am' proclamations occur in John's testimony. There is the 'I Am' that knocks over the detachment of soldiers sent to arrest Jesus:

> Then Jesus, knowing everything that was going to happen, went forward and asked them, 'Who are you looking for?'
>
> They answered Him, 'Jesus from Nazareth.'
>
> Jesus told them, 'I Am.'
>
> Judas, the man who betrayed him, was standing with them.
>
> When Jesus told them, 'I Am,' they backed away and fell to the ground.
>
> John 18:4-6^{ISV}

---

138   https://theopolisinstitute.com/leithart_post/17-and-26/
      (accessed 23 August 2024)

At another time, when He was teaching, He said:

> *'When you have lifted up the Son of Man, then you will know that I Am, and that I do nothing on My own authority. Instead, I speak only what the Father has taught Me.'*
>
> John 8:28^{ISV}

The repeated use of the number 17, from the gospel's opening sentence to the use of the 17th triangular number, 153, in the finale is John's testimony to Jesus as I Am, God Himself.

But it's not just 17 that testifies to I Am, it's also 153. The prophet Isaiah proclaimed the word of God:

> *'This is what the Lord says—your Redeemer, the Holy One of Israel: "I am the Lord your God, who teaches you what is best for you, who directs you in the way you should go.'*
>
> Isaiah 48:17^{NIV}

The words, *'I am the Lord your God'*, in this verse[139] have a gematria of 153. So too does *'He is faithful'* from Numbers 12:7. The phrase, *'the Passover'*, likewise totals 153 in Hebrew, as well as the name of the craftsman, Bezazel,[140] who built the Ark of the Covenant. And as we have seen already, so too do *'sons of God'* and *'He shall cause to inherit'*. Moreover the phrase *'Every place that the sole of your foot will tread upon'* is, with the addition of a kollel, 17 x 153.

Turning to Greek, 153 is the value of *'Rebecca'*, as well as the words we previously noted— *'the Magdalene'* and *'side'*.

---

139 There are many other verses in Scripture with the phrase *'I am the Lord your God'* but most have a numerical value of 193.

140 His name means *in God's shadow* or *in God's protection*. Other Hebrew words totalling 153 are the towns Adadah, *festival* or *border* and Eglayim, *two calves*; as well as 'naganim,' *musicians,* 'mebuqah,' *emptiness*, and Hilkiah, *my portion is Yahweh*.

As the 17th triangular number pointing to both Jesus and the God of Israel, 153 was a wall set up in opposition to the numerical divinities revered by the Pythagoreans.[141] This is the antiphraxis, *obstruction*, being turned on its head and used as a weapon against the beliefs of the Gnostics. In particular, the 4th triangular number, the so-called god-like tetrakys, was under attack. So, too, was the 36th triangular number, 666.

Neither 17 nor 153 were neutral symbols. They were provocative battle banners. John's gospel after all was about the war messiah.

---

141 Besides being the 17th triangular number, 153 equals to the sum of the factorials from 1 to 5. That is, $153 = 1! + 2! + 3! + 4! + 5!$ or $1 + 1\times 2 + 1\times 2\times 3 + 1\times 2\times 3\times 4 + 1\times 2\times 3\times 4\times 5$. Mathematically, it's the total of all possible combination of five things (which, because Python Apollo—after whom Pythagoras was named—was associated with the number 5 and the letter epsilon, with a value of 5, may well have constituted another dig at the Pythagoreans.)

There are many other lovely aspects of 153. To look at just two more: the aliquot factors of 231, the 21st triangular number and a medieval symbol of the Holy Trinity, are 1, 3, 7, 11, 21, 33, 77 and they total 153.

Lastly, to finish with a super simple example: because 153 was the 17th triangular number, it was considered by St. Augustine to represent seven gifts of the Holy Spirit and ten commandments of God and it represented all sorts of people being caught in the gospel 'net'.

PART 9

The next day John saw Jesus coming toward him and said, 'Look, the Lamb of God, who takes away the sin of the world! This is He of whom I said, "A man who comes after me has surpassed me because He was before me." I myself did not know Him, but the reason I came baptising with water was that He might be revealed to Israel.' Then John testified, 'I saw the Spirit descending from heaven like a dove and resting on Him. I myself did not know Him, but the One who sent me to baptise with water told me, "The man on whom you see the Spirit descend and rest is He who will baptise with the Holy Spirit." I have seen and testified that this is the Son of God.' The next day John was there again with two of his disciples. When he saw Jesus walking by, he said, 'Look, the Lamb of God!' And when the two disciples heard him say this, they followed Jesus.

JOHN 1:29-37 BSB

When they had finished eating, Jesus asked Simon Peter,

'Simon son of John, do you love Me more than these?'

'Yes, Lord,' he answered, 'You know I love You.'

Jesus replied, 'Feed My lambs.'

Jesus asked a second time,

'Simon son of John, do you love Me?'

'Yes, Lord,' he answered, 'You know I love You.'

Jesus told him, 'Shepherd My sheep.'

Jesus asked a third time,

'Simon son of John, do you love Me?'

Peter was deeply hurt that Jesus had asked him a third time,

'Do you love Me?'

'Lord, You know all things,' he replied. 'You know I love You.'

Jesus said to him, 'Feed My sheep.

Truly, truly, I tell you, when you were young,

you dressed yourself and walked where you wanted;

but when you are old, you will stretch out your hands,

and someone else will dress you and lead you

where you do not want to go.' Jesus said this to indicate

the kind of death by which Peter would glorify God.

And after He had said this, He told him, 'Follow Me.'

9.1 Recognition and Identification

The opening to John's gospel has a wondrous transition from a vision of the eternal Word at the deep and misty beginning of time through to a definite day anchored in a specific historical moment. That day was Yom Kippur, the Day of Atonement—sometime in autumn in the latter part of the third decade of the first century.[142]

On that day, John the Baptiser was confronted by three questions about his identity. At the same time out in the wilderness, Jesus was being confronted by three tests concerning His identity and destiny as He faced temptation by the devil.[143]

The 'next day', according the gospel account, those questions of identity transition into matters of identification. Dominating the

---

142 If the ministry Jesus began in 30 A.D., Yom Kippur would have been 25 September in the Roman calendar. See cgsf.org/dbeattie/calendar/?roman=30 (accessed 9 December 2021). On the other hand, if His ministry began in 27 A.D., it would have been 29 September. For intervening years, the date of Yom Kippur fell in early October. And for 26 A.D., the date I have come to prefer after reading Christian Gedge's *The Atonement Clock*, it was 9 October just after the beginning of a Jubilee year. This will be explained in the second book in this series, which explores many inter-related aspects of time in relation to the first sign—or miracle—of Jesus.

143 A few years later, again on the Day of Atonement, Jesus raised the question of His own identity when He was with His disciples at Caesarea Philippi.

rest of the first chapter are themes of recognition and identification, culminating in a call to follow. These are also major themes of the last chapter.

At the beginning, John the Baptiser not only recognises Jesus coming toward Him but identifies Him as the Lamb of God.

At the end, John the apostle not only recognises Jesus on the shore but identifies Him as the Lord. 'It is the Lord!'[144]

At the beginning, Jesus looks for Philip and says, 'Follow Me.'[145] At the end, He pursues Simon Peter and issues Him the same call: 'Follow Me.'[146]

In the opening scenes there is a 'season'—extending from the Day of Atonement through the Feast of Tabernacles—about identity and identification, and stretching into the miracle at Cana in the second chapter.

When Jesus returned from the desert, the Baptiser identified Him as the Lamb of God. The next day, he identified Him as One on whom the Spirit rested like a dove. The following day, he identified Him once again as the Lamb of God. These three identifications are paralleled, in the final scene, by the three questions of Jesus that are followed by implicit identifications of Peter as a shepherd—no longer a fisherman.

Just as Elijah had turned back from his calling, so Simon Peter had been tempted to go back to fishing. However, Jesus, the Good Shepherd, had come after him to move him on from 'fisher of men' to an appointment as an under-shepherd in the kingdom of heaven. The mantle of Elijah was Peter's, if he would accept it.

---

144 John 21:7
145 John 1:43
146 John 21:18

Just before Elijah was taken up to heaven, a 'fire from heaven' incident occurs involving the number 153. Not fish, admittedly, but men.

King Ahab had died and his son Ahaziah had taken the throne. He'd had a serious accident on falling through a window lattice. Sending messengers to Baal-zebub, *lord of the flies*, an idol worshipped by the Philistines at Ekron, Ahaziah asked if he'd recover from his injuries. Elijah intercepted the messengers and sent them back with a dire prophecy.[147] Ahaziah then sent a troop of fifty men with a captain to bring Elijah in. As the squad approached Elijah, fire from heaven came down and consumed them. A second troop of fifty men with a captain was sent to bring Elijah in. As before, fire fell from heaven and consumed them. A third squad was sent. This time, the captain—the 153rd man—humbly approached Elijah, pleading for mercy. Elijah accompanied the captain back to the king and pronounced Ahaziah's doom.[148] This was the last major recorded incident before his ascension in a whirlwind.

Similarly, the story of Jesus on the beach and the haul of 153 fish is the last major incident recorded in His life on earth before His ascension.

The fire from heaven that featured so strongly in so many Elijah episodes was still to come in the story of Jesus—ten days after the Ascension at the time of Pentecost.

---

147 This part of the story also fits the theme of recognition. Ahaziah quizzes the messengers about the appearance of the man who sent them back the way they'd come. On hearing about a garment of hair and a leather belt, Ahaziah immediately identified Elijah. John the Baptiser dressed in a similar eccentric way with a garment of camel hair and a leather belt.

148 2 Kings 1:1–18. Does this story fit the pattern of inheritance associated with 153? If we consider that one aspect of inheritance is the possible loss of it, yes, then it does. Ahaziah reigned only two years and left no posterity. His brother Jehoram then became king.

9.2 Lambs of God

The Lamb of God identified by John the Baptiser becomes, in the progressive unveiling of the gospel narrative, both the Good Shepherd and the Gate of the Sheep. In the last scene, the Shepherd appoints an under-shepherd whose duties include the feeding of 'lambs'—the children of God, the brothers and sisters of the Lord.

The Aramaic word for *lamb* is 'ṭāle'—but that's also the word for *young man*. It's a lovely pun. Because 'Lamb of God' also means 'Man of God'. There are several different Hebrew words for *lamb* but the one corresponding to 'ṭāle' is 'tela', which is found in the prophecy of Isaiah:

> *Behold, the Lord God will come with might,*
> *With His arm ruling for Him.*
> *Behold, His compensation is with Him,*
> *And His reward before Him.*
> *Like a shepherd He will tend His flock,*
> *In His arm He will gather the lambs*
> *And carry them in the fold of His robe;*
> *He will gently lead the nursing ewes.*
>
> Isaiah 40:10–11[NASB]

The expression 'the fold of His robe' means 'His bosom'. As previously noted, when Jesus said to Simon Peter, *'You dressed yourself,'* He used the word for putting on a girdle or pulling up the slack on clothing —an action that created the folds of a 'bosom'.

Jesus was prophesying that, even in his death, Peter was safe in the Father's bosom. His words immediately prior were 'Feed My sheep' and this combination—lambs, shepherd, sheep, bosom—was surely meant to evoke Isaiah's comforting promise of compensation and reward.

However, yet again, there are also echoes of Elijah here. The 'man of God' pun reminds us that this is the title used three times as an honorific for Elijah when the squadrons of fifty men and their captains come to round him up at Ahaziah's command. Twice Elijah responds:

> *'If I am a man of God, let fire come down from heaven and destroy you and your fifty men!'*
>
> 2 Kings 1:10;12[NLT]

And the fire fell.

9.3 Doubly Forgiven

ALTHOUGH JOHN THE GOSPEL WRITER made a point of numbering the 153 fish caught in the net, in actual fact there are 154 fish in this scene by the lake. Jesus already had bread and fish cooking on the breakfast coals.

So what is the significance of the extra fish? The most obvious answer is that 154 is twice 77. This is a number that first appears when Cain's great-great-great grandson says to his wives:

> 'Adah and Zillah, listen to me; wives of Lamech, hear my words. I have killed a man for wounding me, a young man for injuring me. If Cain is avenged seven times, then Lamech seventy-seven times.'
>
> Genesis 4:23–24[NIV]

From the very earliest times, the number 77 was associated with vengeance and retaliation, with payback and reprisal—multiplied many times over.

But then, in the hands of Jesus, that notion was entirely overturned. It is no coincidence that the moment of inversion involved Simon Peter.

> *Peter came up and said to him, 'Lord, how often will my brother sin against me, and I forgive him? As many as seven times?'*
>
> *Jesus said to him, 'I do not say to you seven times, but seventy-seven[149] times.'*
>
> Matthew 18:21–22^{ESV}

That answer would have been so startling to Peter that he would never have forgotten it. The 'measure of the fish' is 153, but the 'measure of forgiveness' is 77. Thus 154, being twice 77, suggests *double forgiveness*—forgiveness for the betrayal in the courtyard of Caiaphas and also forgiveness for turning aside from his calling.

Peter's reinstatement does not mean he never stumbles again in his faith. Far from it. In a few short months, he would show immense courage in defending the name of Jesus before the Sanhedrin. Yet he would later flip-flop in his faith, and—perhaps not surprisingly—it was to be to over the question of the nature of the 'fish in the net'. Or, to put it more accurately, the 'creatures in the sail'.

---

149 As we have previously seen (Section 3.2), there was considerable ambiguity in both Greek and Hebrew regarding mathematical operations. 70 + 7 could also have been 70 x 7, so some translations render this as seventy times seven, not seventy-seven.

9.4 The Sail and the Net

> *Peter remained for a considerable time at Jaffa, staying at the house of a man called Simon, a tanner...*
>
> *About noon Peter went up on the house-top to pray. He had become unusually hungry and wished for food; but, while they were preparing it, he fell into a trance. The sky had opened to his view, and what seemed to be an enormous sail was descending, being let down to the earth by ropes at the four corners. In it were all kinds of quadrupeds, reptiles and birds, and a voice came to him which said, 'Rise, Peter, kill and eat.'*
>
> *'On no account, Lord,' he replied; 'for I have never yet eaten anything unholy and impure.'*
>
> *Again a second time a voice was heard which said, 'What God has purified, you must not regard as unholy.'*
>
> *This was said three times, and immediately the sail was drawn up out of sight.*
>
> Acts 9:43; 10:9–16^{WEY}

SIMON BAR JONAH, OTHERWISE KNOWN AS Cephas or Peter was staying in Joppa,[150] a town whose enduring fame in Scripture came from its association with his father's namesake, the prophet Jonah. It was in Joppa that Jonah—who, like Peter, was from Galilee[151]—found a ship going to Tarshish.

---

150 Also known in English as 'Jaffa'.

151 Jonah was from Gath-hepher in Galilee. Thus the Jewish leaders were incorrect in saying to Nicodemus: *'Search the Scriptures and see for yourself—no prophet ever comes from Galilee!'* (John 7:52^{NLT}) Though perhaps they considered, as some do, that Jonah cannot be classed as a prophet since his foretelling of the doom of Nineveh did not come to pass.

Jonah's calling was to preach to the Gentiles—specifically to the Assyrians of Nineveh who would eventually become the pitiless rulers of his homeland—but instead he was on the run. He turned his back on God's summons and was intent on sailing as far as he could in the opposite direction.

Here, in Peter's story, we have an exemplar of a 'healing of history'. Jesus had continually modeled this activity[152] and now, as His representative, Peter was to carry on a similar work. He was called to the same vocation as Jonah and to repair the spiritual fissures he had caused. Tarshish was the 'ends of the earth' in Jonah's time, and he'd headed there to avoid preaching repentance to the Gentile rulers of his nation—because, so he eventually reveals, he couldn't face the prospect that God was about to show mercy and favour to the people of Nineveh.

Jonah was so furious that he upended God's love, turning it into an accusation of injustice:

> *Lord, isn't this what I said while I was still in my home country? That's why I fled previously to Tarshish, because I knew You're a compassionate God, slow to anger, overflowing with gracious love, and reluctant to send trouble.*
>
> Jonah 4:2^{ISV}

Jonah was quoting God's own words about Himself when He had allowed Moses a vision of His back as He passed by while Moses was covered within a cleft in the rock. But Jonah blatantly omitted a critical word from this description: that of *faithfulness* or *truth*.

In the Middle Ages, one of the most popular themes for plays and poems was based around the notion of the 'Four Daughters of

---

[152] See the series *Jesus and the Healing of History*—#1 *Like Wildflowers, Suddenly*; #2 *Bent World, Bright Wings*; #3 *Silk Shadows, Rings of God*; #4 *Where His Feet Pass*; #5 *The Singing Silence*—for details of how, in various different locations, Jesus was not only healing people but also the history of the land.

God'. It originated in a Jewish teaching of the first century which recognised the inherent opposition between mercy and justice, between truth and kindness—yet also realised they could come together in divine harmony:

> *Mercy and truth have met together;*
> *Righteousness and peace have kissed.*
>
> Psalm 85:10^{NKJV}

Justice and truth are natural allies, as are mercy and kindness—but the pairs are also innately hostile to one another. Only within God's own nature can they find perfect and paradoxical expression.

So there was Peter in Joppa. He was faced with the same prospect as Jonah had been. God had sent him a vision of a sail—in many versions, a 'sheet'—full of unclean beasts and birds. While he was still pondering the meaning of the revelation, three men arrived from a centurion named Cornelius who'd also had a vision. An angel told Cornelius to send to Joppa for a man named Simon Peter who was staying by the sea with a tanner named Simon. On arriving, Peter told the messengers:

> *'I am the Simon you are inquiring for. What is the reason of your coming?'*
>
> *Their reply was, 'Cornelius, a Captain, an upright and God-fearing man, of whom the whole Jewish nation speaks well, has been divinely instructed by a holy angel to send for you to come to his house and listen to what you have to say.'*
>
> Acts 10:21–22WEY

At the moment of choice, that moment when Jonah had said, 'No!' when God asked him to preach to the brutal Gentile invaders of his land, Peter chose instead to say, 'Yes!' He went with the messengers who invited him to preach to a representative of the brutal Gentile invaders in his own time.

And so began the incoming of the Gentiles when, at the preaching of the Good News, the Holy Spirit fell on Cornelius and his household.

We might be tempted to think Peter would be permanently affected by this moment and always welcome Gentile believers. But, as it turned out years later, he was not always consistent in his approach. Paul describes a confrontation between himself and Peter:

> *When Cephas came to Antioch, however, I opposed him to his face, because he stood to be condemned. For before certain men came from James, he used to eat with the Gentiles. But when they arrived, he began to draw back and separate himself, for fear of those in the circumcision group. The other Jews joined him in his hypocrisy, so that by their hypocrisy even Barnabas was led astray.*
>
> Galatians 2:11–13[BSB]

The people-pleasing fears of Peter, the under-shepherd, had so defiled the wider flock that he to be forcibly reminded by Paul, the under-rower,[153] that Jesus had *'other sheep too that are not in this sheepfold... there will be one flock with one shepherd.'*

John 10:16[NLT]

The 'net' which held the 153 fish representing the *children of God* became in Peter's vision the 'sail' or 'sheet' representing the full diversity of nations.

> *For God so loved the world that He gave His one and only Son...*
>
> John 3:16[NIV]

---

153 See 1 Corinthians 4:1 where the Greek for *servant* derives from *under-rower* and may refer to the Temple Guard.

9.5 The Long-Awaited Anointing

Jesus said to Simon Peter, 'Simon, son of Jonah, do you love Me more than these?'

John 21:15^{NKJV}

If we think for a moment, Jesus picks a very curious form of address when He says, 'Simon, son of Jonah.' It's not Peter, not Cephas, not Simon plain and simple, but specifically reinforced three times: 'Simon, son of Jonah.' Now as we've just seen, the sudden mention of Jonah sets up for a healing of history to occur later at Joppa.

Still, why reference Jonah at that particular moment? Why suddenly insert an explicit reference to Jonah in a scene jam-packed with subtle allusions to Elijah? Isn't it a distraction?

Actually, no. The repeated mention of Jonah underscores that the scene is indeed about the passing of Elijah's mantle.

In Jewish tradition, the legacy of Elisha—the prophet who received Elijah's mantle—passed to Jonah. In fact, Jonah was understood to have carried out one of the tasks that Elijah was asked by God to undertake—the anointing of Jehu as king of Israel.

> *Now Elisha the prophet summoned one of the sons of the prophets and said to him, 'Get ready and take this flask of oil in your hand, and go to Ramoth-gilead. When you arrive there, then look there for Jehu the son of Jehoshaphat the son of Nimshi, and go in and have him get up from among his brothers, and bring him to an inner room. Then take the flask of oil and pour it on his head, and say, "This is what the Lord says: 'I have anointed you king over Israel.'" Then open the door and flee, and do not wait.'*
>
> 2 Kings 9:1–3[NASB]

In this historical record, the young prophet who anointed Jehu is anonymous. Tradition, however, identified him as Jonah—in his youth, long before he was called to prophesy to the people of Nineveh.[154] I believe the tradition is correct precisely because Jesus addresses Simon as 'son of Jonah' during the breakfast when Elijah's mantle was being handed on. In doing so, Jesus is setting Simon up to finish the task that Elijah, Elisha and Jonah had all baulked at completing.

Nine centuries prior to the breakfast by the lake, Elijah had mentored Elisha and passed his mantle on to him as his God-appointed chosen successor. Elisha in turn had mentored Jonah, effectively handing on Elijah's mantle to the young prophet destined to be the only one asked to preach directly to the Gentiles.[155] Now we don't know who carried the mantle between the time of Jonah and John the Baptiser—perhaps there was no one.[156] Possibly it was waiting to be activated once more when

---

154 See, for example, chabad.org/library/article_cdo/aid/463982/jewish/The-Prophet-Jonah.htm (accessed 12 August 2022)

155 Obadiah and Nahum prophesied about the Gentiles but there is no indication that they preached to them.

156 The name, Jonah, is sometimes translated 'John'—so perhaps we have a clue here that when the angel directed Zechariah to call his son 'John', it was a summoning of the mantle of Elijah, last held by Jonah.

John returned to the Brook Cherith. Certainly the words 'son of Jonah' from Jesus convey the strong impression that it's been dormant since the time of Jonah.

Now Elijah, as we have seen, didn't obey God's instructions to anoint either Jehu or Hazael. Neither did Elisha. In fact Elisha met with Hazael in Damascus and informed him he would be king[157] but he did not take the opportunity to anoint him. As for Jehu, although he had to wait at least 21 years—and possibly as many as 37—he did eventually get anointed to rule the northern kingdom of Israel when Elisha sent Jonah off with instructions to do it as swiftly as possible.

We tend to think of Jonah as the only prophet who strenuously defied God, but in fact he was following in the footsteps of some serious role models. Apparently he was the third generation prophet unwilling to obey God's commands concerning the Gentiles. After all, it was the Gentile commander Hazael whom neither Elijah nor Elisha could apparently bring themselves to anoint—*ever*. The appointment of Jehu, an Israelite, took decades but at least it happened eventually.[158]

The anointing of Hazael by a prophet of Yahweh could have been a turning point. A Gentile king who recognised the Lord's authorisation of his coming to power would very likely have sought Yahweh's favour through worship and devotion. God

---

157 He was to replace Ben-Hadad, *son of the storm-god*. Hazael, *God has seen* or *vision of God*, has a name suggesting a new ruler in the natural realm as well as in a spiritual sense.

158 Just as Elisha met with Hazael and did not make the most of the chance to anoint him, so Elijah met up with Jehu and also let the opportunity slip. This becomes clear from a remark of Jehu to his aide and chariot officer, Bidkar in 2 Kings 9:25-26. Jehu reminds Bidkar that they both witnessed the prophecy given to Ahab regarding the consequences of the theft of Naboth's vineyard and the murder of his sons. Since that prophecy was given by Elijah, it is clear Elijah failed, at least fifteen years previously and perhaps as much as thirty years previously to make the most of the encounter God had arranged.

wanted the incoming of the Gentiles to His kingdom but, one by one, the great and famous prophets of old had failed to extend the invitation. Jonah had had a hissy fit in Nineveh when God chose to the merciful to the city after the people repented. He wanted Nineveh destroyed and was incredibly dismayed at the humble response of the city elders to His preaching of doom. It seems that, like Elijah and Elisha, he too wasted the golden opportunity presented to him—he didn't follow up on any of the people and instruct them about Yahweh.[159]

Centuries had come and gone since the days of Elijah, Elisha and Jonah. And God still wanted the Gentiles as part of His kingdom. He was still waiting for the anointing He had commissioned to take place.

In giving Elijah's mantle to Peter, Jesus also gave him Jonah's mantle. After all, it was the same thing. And Jesus made it clear that He was passing on the mantle through His carefully chosen words. His agenda, in retrospect, is obvious. He handed over the mantle in order to set up the perfect opportunity for Jonah's unfinished task to be completed. Of course, a lakeside in Galilee wasn't the perfect location. That would have to wait until Peter went to Joppa—the location where Jonah sailed off to the end of the known world. Still, everything hinged on Peter choosing differently from Jonah when it became apparent to him the task of preaching to the Gentiles was his. God will

---

[159] Imagine the long-term outcome if he had followed up his announcement with preaching about Yahweh! If Jonah was indeed a protégé of Elisha, then they both lived before the Assyrian invasion of the northern kingdom of Israel. That puts them in the time period before the Assyrian conquest. The rise of Nineveh was beginning but it had not yet culminated in the most brutal empire of the ancient world. The people of Nineveh, the Assyrians, had showed a willingness to respond to Jonah's preaching but he did not capitalise on it. He was so offended by God's mercy that he failed to realise it was not for the Assyrians alone—it was actually part of His desire to extend mercy to the people of Israel by forestalling an invasion in the years to come.

not violate free will. But He certainly had to pull out all stops in the persuasion department.

A Roman centurion had a vision of an angel who told him to send to Joppa for Peter. Like Hazael, Cornelius was an officer in a foreign army oppressing the land of Israel—but, more than that, his experience evokes Hazael's name with its meaning *vision of God*. This isn't simply any Gentile but one who should specifically remind us of Hazael.

Even though Peter headed off with the centurion's servants to meet Cornelius, he still displayed considerable prejudice. He'd been with Jesus when the Samaritans welcomed Him so he should have done better when it came to courtesy towards his host. Nevertheless, to give him his due, he did manage to outline the gospel. It was enough. The Holy Spirit immediately intervened in a descent of grace. The anointing that so many prophets had failed to bring about was accomplished by God Himself.

The mission to the Gentiles, delayed by centuries, so long awaited by God, was finally underway.

Jesus turned and saw them following.
What do you want? He asked.
They said to Him, Rabbi (which means Teacher),
where are You staying?
Come and see, He replied.
So they went and saw where He was staying,
and spent that day with Him. It was about the tenth hour.
Andrew, Simon Peter's brother, was one of the two
who heard John's testimony and followed Jesus.
He first found his brother Simon and told him,
We have found the Messiah (which is translated as Christ).
Andrew brought him to Jesus, who looked at him and said,
You are Simon son of John. You will be called Cephas
(which is translated as Peter).
The next day Jesus decided to set out for Galilee.
Finding Philip, He told him, Follow Me.
Now Philip was from Bethsaida,
the same town as Andrew and Peter.
Philip found Nathanael...

JOHN
1:38 -45 BSB

PART

Later, by the Sea of Tiberias,
Jesus again revealed Himself to the disciples.
He made Himself known in this way:
Simon Peter, Thomas called Didymus,
Nathanael from Cana in Galilee, the sons of Zebedee,
and two other disciples were together.
Simon Peter told them, 'I am going fishing.'
'We will go with you,' they said.
So they went out and got into the boat,
but caught nothing that night.
Early in the morning, Jesus stood on the shore,
but the disciples did not recognise that it was Jesus.
So He called out to them,
'Children, do you have any fish?'
'No,' they answered.

JOHN
21: 1-5
BSB

TEN

10.1 Recognition

THE TIME SIGNATURES AT THE beginning of John's gospel are very clear. *The next day... the next day... the next day... on the third day*. The date-stamps move the story from the Day of Atonement towards the Feast of Tabernacles.

Now this week continued the season of identity and identification begun when John the Baptiser pointed out the Lamb of God. That had happened on the day after Yom Kippur. On the very next day, he did it for a second time. Hearing that identification, two disciples—one of whom was Andrew—took notice and began following Jesus. In quick succession they identified Jesus as 'Rabbi' and, by the end of the day, as the Messiah.

By four o'clock in the afternoon, Andrew had made up his mind. He took off[160] to find his brother Simon and to tell him he'd found the Christ, *the anointed one*, the Messiah. It's a little strange that Andrew didn't ever get the credit for recognising this straight out of the gate—it's Simon who receives this acknowledgment.

---

160 As the hour of prayer finished.

That happened a few years later—on another Yom Kippur—when Jesus named him 'Cephas' or 'Peter'.[161]

Yet, perhaps it's not so strange. Andrew told his brother Simon; he didn't actually confess it to Jesus Himself. He didn't create the opportunity for a name exchange[162] with Jesus that Simon did later.

Yet the moment Jesus saw Simon He informed him of his new identity. Even though it would not come to pass for a few years. It was a prophetic pledge of a future that was still to mature.

As we saw previously,[163] Cephas is essentially the same as Caiaphas—the High Priest. It means *rock*, but that bald definition misses the nuances behind it all. The Greek name 'petros' has overtones of *a rock from which an enterprise is started*—a stone wharf where a voyage starts; a foundation stone for a building. The Hebrew word 'peter' denotes the *firstborn, the one who opens*

---

161 It's most likely to be two or three years later. Some scholars suggest Jesus preached on the 'Spirit of the Lord' in Nazareth at Yom Kippur. This would mean that the temptation in the wilderness occurred on the first Yom Kippur during Jesus' ministry; the announcement at Nazareth on the second Yom Kippur, and the confession of Simon at Caesarea Philippi on the third or fourth Yom Kippur. If however Christian Gedge's 'Atonement clock' is right, then the announcement at Nazareth would be after the end of a Jubilee year not at the beginning or in the middle of it—assuming that it is on Yom Kippur. However, this reading is not customary, at least today, for Yom Kippur. If we align it with present custom, another possibility is that Jesus is reading it on the very last Sabbath of the Jubilee Year. The beginning of Isaiah 61 is no longer read in synagogues. It is not known when the decision was made to exclude the first nine verses and start at the tenth for the reading of the weekly portion, but it was after it became well-known that Jesus had used these verses to point to Himself in His hometown. The rest of Isaiah 61 as well as all of 62 and also 63 as far as verse 9 is read on the 51st week of the Jewish year, on the Sabbath before Rosh Hashanah, the beginning of the New Year. This is the latest possible time it could be read and still be within the Jubilee Year calculated by Christian Gedge. It is also the only time it could be read on the correct date for such portions.

162 See: Anne Hamilton, *Name Covenant: Invitation to Friendship*, Armour Books 2018, for the significance of name exchanges in Scripture.

163 Section 7.4

the way. The Hebrew 'cephas', on the other hand, has resonances of a *cornerstone*, of *atonement*, of the *covering* on the mercy seat within the Holy of Holies, of the *palm* of a hand and the *frond* of a palm tree, of the *sole* of a foot.

From the moment Jesus met Simon, He designated him as the heir—the one to carry the 'family' mantle. The Lamb of God was the bellwether sheep, the leader, who was beginning to gather the first sheep of an immense worldwide flock. Yet the Lamb was also the Good Shepherd and, from the first, He prepared those who would be His successors to be shepherds in their turn.

10.2 Bethsaida

Andrew, Simon and Philip all came from Bethsaida, a town on the shores of the Lake of the Harp—the Kinnereth—which throughout the gospels is called the Lake of Tiberias or the Sea of Galilee. Later in John's gospel, Andrew and Philip will appear again together during a conversation just prior to the 'sign' of the multiplied loaves and fishes. It's from Luke's gospel we learn that this miracle happened in the solitary region just outside Bethsaida.[164]

Bethsaida means *house of the fisherman* or *house of the hunter*. A thousand years before the time of Jesus, it had been part of the independent kingdom of Geshur. David had married a princess of Geshur—Maacah, daughter of Talmai—and with her had become the father of Absalom. Geshur, *the land of bridges*, was the safe haven where Absalom fled after killing his older brother, Amnon. It was there, in his grandfather's realm, that Absalom conceived his plan for rebellion against his father and the overthrow of David's throne.

John brings the first faint whiff of revolution to the fore with this mention of Bethsaida. In the background, there is perhaps a waft of the same idea. Remember—the day before this fateful meeting, Jesus had emerged from wilderness and appeared back

---

[164] Luke 9:10

at Bethany-beyond-the-Jordan. He would have had to have walked through Gilead to get there—and there is a reasonable chance He came through the region of the ancient and sinister Forest of Ephraim on the way. Absalom was killed in this locality when his long, luxuriant hair became caught in a tree.

John's implied question is: who will this latterday 'Son of David' turn out to be? A rebel against authority, like Absalom? In many ways, the popularity of Jesus had the same kind of ring to it as that of Absalom. After all the people, particularly after the free feed on the outskirts of Bethsaida, wanted to make Him king. They were looking for accessibility, along with wise and natural justice in a ruler. Just as Absalom had provided that in a previous age, Jesus did so in His own. But there the resemblance ended. Jesus resisted the popular desire to make Him king—perhaps to show that the royal messiah was there to heal another old wound in the history of the land: the civil war that Absalom brought to pass through an illegitimate use of power.

10.3 THE 'FIVE'

DAVID HAD 'THE THREE'—THE mighty men Jashobeam, Eleazar and Shammah. In addition there were Abishai and Benaiah who were as famous and battle-tested as 'The Three' but not counted in their number.[165] So there were The Three plus two other equally renowned warriors.

Likewise, Jesus has 'The Three'—Peter, James and John—but this special group has not made its full appearance as the gospel opens. Nevertheless it does feature *five*. To start with, there are Andrew, Simon, Philip, Nathanael and an unnamed disciple who is almost certainly the apostle John himself. At the end, in similar fashion, there are Simon Peter, Thomas, Nathanael, the sons of Zebedee and two other unnamed disciples. Although there are seven in total, they are grouped as *five*.

The interesting aspect of this is that, in Scripture, groups of *five* are characteristic of women, not men. Exodus, the second book in the Torah, opens with the exploits of five women who are instrumental in saving the life of Moses. Numbers, the second last book of the Torah, ends with five women creating a new precedent for inheritance. These groups of five are arranged in basically the same position at both the front and back of the Torah—just as

---

165 2 Samuel 23:8–23

John has arranged his five groups of disciples in the same position back and front of his gospel.

However he's not the only one to highlight *five*. The first chapter of Matthew mentions five women within the genealogy of Jesus. And, although the information is scattered and the exact number of women who made their way to the tomb and were witnesses to the resurrection of Jesus is uncertain, the most likely answer appears to be five.[166]

Importantly, the majority of these women are named. They are not anonymous. Back in Exodus, there are the midwives, Shiphrah and Puah, as well as the mother and sister of Moses, Jochebed and Miriam respectively. Lastly there's Pharaoh's daughter whose identity is never unveiled in any of the five books of the Torah but is named as Bithiah in the genealogical record of Chronicles.

Matthew's gospel lists Tamar, Rahab, Ruth, and rather strangely 'Uriah's wife' instead of Bathsheba, then lastly, Mary the mother of Jesus.

The account of the resurrection is either the last, or close to the last, event mentioned in any gospel. By combining the information in the varying reports, we can conclude that there were probably five women who took spices to the tomb of Jesus on the morning of the resurrection: Mary Magdalene, Mary the mother of James, Salome, Joanna and at least one unnamed other.

There are still further sets of five females. Although there were many women who prophesied and whose names are given in the biblical record, there are only five who are actually designated as

---

166 Present at the crucifixion were *'many women'*—from the varying descriptions somewhere between four and seven: Mary the mother of Jesus, Mary Magdalene, Mary the mother of James and Joseph, Salome who may be 'the mother of the sons of Zebedee', the sister or sister-in-law of Jesus' mother who may be 'Mary of Clopas'.

prophets, at least in the Hebrew portion of the Scriptures: these are Miriam, Deborah, Huldah, Noadiah and 'the prophetess' who was married to Isaiah. Likewise, there are five barren women who eventually gave birth and who are mentioned there: Sarah, Rebekah, Rachel, Hannah and the wife of Manoah who was also the mother of Samson.[167]

A mysterious grace-thread of 'five women' runs all through Scripture. John seems have deliberately but subtly evoked this concept while also preparing to introduce *five* women who will be strongly featured in his account.[168]

---

[167] Michal may also have been barren. It's unclear whether she was infertile or whether David simply refused to have anything to do with her after she confronted him about his shameless dancing—his nakedness before the Ark of the Covenant was in violation of God's direction in Exodus 20:26. There's also considerable ambiguity as to whether she had children by her husband Paltiel. Elizabeth is another woman who was barren but she too eventually gave birth; however she is not included in this count because her story is not part of the Hebrew portion of the Scriptures.

[168] Seven women are mentioned in total, but two of them—Jesus' aunt, and the wife of Clopas—do not have speaking roles. The five who do are (1) Mary, the mother of Jesus; (2) the woman at the well at Sychar; (3) the woman caught in adultery; (4) Mary Magdalene; (5) Martha.

John 1:45 BSB

Philip found Nathanael and told him, 'We have found the One Moses wrote about in the Law, the One the prophets foretold— Jesus of Nazareth, the son of Joseph.'

John 20:30–31 BSB

Jesus performed many other signs in the presence of His disciples, which are not written in this book. But these are written so that you may believe that Jesus is the Christ, the Son of God, and that by believing you may have life in His name.

11.1 The Writings

> *Jesus performed many other signs in the presence of His disciples, which are not written in this book. But these are written so that you may believe that Jesus is the Christ, the Son of God, and that by believing you may have life in His name.*
>
> John 20:30–31 [BSB]

Many scholars incline towards the belief that these lines are the true end of the fourth gospel and that all of chapter 21 forms an appendix—an epilogue later added by another writer. However, given the strength and abundance of the chiastic links between the first and last chapters, I personally find it impossible to believe that they were not conceived of as a single unity.

Certainly these last two verses of chapter 20 have a 'feel' of a final statement, but that's to look at them through the lens of our culture—not through the mind of a Hebrew writer intent on pairing up each and every aspect of his testimony so that every statement is verified by a second and independent witness.

At the beginning, John reports the words of Philip to Nathanael, thereby proclaiming Jesus as the One Moses wrote about, the One the prophets foretold, Jesus of Nazareth and the Son of Joseph. At the end, John then goes on to complement these claims by adding that Jesus is also the Christ and the Son of God.

In the opening narrative, the Baptiser had just denied being Elijah, dismissed the notion he was the Prophet and rejected the idea he was the Messiah. But, in short order, the Apostle has identified Jesus as both the Prophet and the Messiah. He was the 'new Moses'—the promised law-giver and deliverer:

> 'The Lord your God will raise up for you a prophet like me from among you, from your fellow Israelites. You must listen to him.'
>
> Deuteronomy 18:15^{NIV}

The Father Himself identifies Jesus as the fulfillment of this prophecy when He quotes this very line from the Torah during the Transfiguration:

> 'This is My beloved Son, in whom I am well pleased. Listen to Him.'
>
> Matthew 17:5^{WEB}

We are unused to thinking of Jesus as a law-giver, yet He was. Furthermore, when we contrast Jesus with Moses, we discover that Moses was comparatively lenient and easygoing.

'Don't kill,' Moses said.

> 'Don't even get angry,' Jesus said. 'It's murder of the heart.'[169]

'Don't commit adultery,' Moses said.

> 'Don't even think a lustful thought,' said Jesus. 'That's adultery of the heart.'

'Don't steal,' Moses said.

---

[169] Although Jesus doesn't say exactly this in Matthew 5:21–22, it's what He implies.

'Give to those who ask,' said Jesus. 'Don't turn your back on someone who wants to borrow from you.'

'Don't seek revenge,' said Moses. 'Don't bear a grudge. Love your neighbour as yourself.'

'Love your enemies,' said Jesus. 'Do good to those who hate you.'

We tend to think of grace—the grace and truth of Jesus—as proceeding from His divine compassion for our human weakness. That results in a tolerant, forgiving view on His part of our proclivity towards sin. But that's not the case at all. Yes, it's true that His grace proceeds from His divine compassion for our human weakness but not for a moment does He indulge our sinful attitudes. Rather His lovingkindness towards us results in a grace-gift of empowering strength to *overcome* our proclivity towards sin.

Jesus did not lower the bar on the keeping of the Law, He raised to an unimaginable degree. In the lead-up to this pronouncement that the Ten Commandments are a *minimum* requirement, not the supreme gold standard, He was very clear He did not come to overturn the Law:

> *Don't misunderstand why I have come. I did not come to abolish the law of Moses or the writings of the prophets. No, I came to accomplish their purpose. I tell you the truth, until heaven and earth disappear, not even the smallest detail of God's law will disappear until its purpose is achieved.*
>
> Matthew 5:17–18^{NLT}

John's mirror-placed comments loudly proclaim Jesus as the One who accomplished this unique fulfillment.

11.2 Son of Joseph

Jesus did not merely fulfill the Law and the prophets. He fulfilled tradition too. We have already noted some of these: the Messiah would be identified by Moses and Elijah.[170] Tick that box at the Transfiguration.

Moreover, He also fulfilled the expectation about the coming of the Four Craftsmen. He embodied the royal Messiah, to be called 'Son of David'; as well as a war messiah to be known as 'Son of Joseph'; a priestly messiah like Melchizedek; and the prophet like Elijah as prophesied at the end of the book of Malachi.

Matthew, Mark and Luke all use the term 'Son of David'—17 times, of course!—as a title to describe Jesus but John does not.[171] On the other hand, John uses the phrase 'Son of Joseph' to describe Jesus while the other evangelists do not.[172] This seems to suggest that one of John's aims in writing his gospel was to present Jesus as the war messiah.

---

170 Succoth 5a in Talmud; Deuteronomy Midrash Rabbah 3. 239b

171 In John 7:42[NIV], the people ask, '*Does not Scripture say that the Messiah will come from David's descendants and from Bethlehem, the town where David lived?*' However, this is not the specific term 'Son of David' as a messianic title. In fact, the Greek says, 'seed of David'.

172 Luke uses it in the genealogy of Jesus, but again, it is not a messianic title.

This is not to suggest John ignored the claims of Jesus as the royal messiah—in fact, he adds a kingship scene absent from the other gospels. However he seems to avoid using the 'Son of David' title so as not to diffuse his focus.

The 'Son of Joseph' was also called 'Son of Ephraim'. This was in line with the expectation that the war messiah would be from the tribe of Joseph through his younger son, the patriarch Ephraim. There is only one reference to Ephraim throughout the gospels and epistles. It's a passing mention in John 11:54 where it's recorded that, after raising Lazarus from the dead, Jesus stopped His public ministry and withdrew to the wilderness village of Ephraim to escape the attention of the authorities.

Did that sojourn in some way entitle Him to say He was a 'son of Ephraim'? There is no question that, although He fulfilled various traditions, He also defied expectations in the way He did so. Matthew recalls the foster-father of Jesus settling in Nazareth and thus satisfying the prophecy:

> 'He will be called a Nazarene.'
>
> Matthew 2:23[NLT]

Where this prophecy comes from is anyone's guess. It's not found anywhere in the canonical Hebrew Scriptures. However, it may simply be an oral tradition. We should not discount it just because that's the most likely answer. It's wise to be careful that our respect for the Word of God does not become idolatry of the written word. When we disdain 'tradition' as unbiblical, it's all too often at the cost of multiplying our own versions of ritual and custom. Jesus respected tradition and continually used it to point to Himself:

- In addition to the traditions surrounding the Four Craftsmen, He also fulfilled the tradition that it would be possible to identify the Messiah because He would cast out demons—and the sure sign would be His ability to cast out dumb demons.[173]

- He further fulfilled the tradition of re-affirming covenant at Shechem, the first place Abram made an altar on entering Canaan.

- In the lead-up to Hanukkah, *the festival of lights* and a human tradition to celebrate a great victory by the Maccabees, Jesus made the statement, *'I am the light of the world.'* Also in relation to the Maccabees, His triumphal entry into Jerusalem was similar to the way they were greeted with waving palm branches.[174]

- He fulfilled the tradition of the 'season of repentance' for the forty days leading up to Yom Kippur.[175] This was the period when He fasted in the wilderness.

- His first miracle seems to have coincided with the ancient Canaanite festival of New Wine, as much as it did with the 'Days of Joyfully Drawing Water' during the week of the Feast of Tabernacles.

These instances are unlikely to be all.[175]

---

173 There are no instances of exorcism in the Hebrew Scriptures. The 'casting out' of demons is first mentioned in the gospels. It was understood that one of the signs of the Messiah's coming would be His ability to routinely and easily cast out demons, particularly the dumb ones who could not be compelled to reveal their names and thus give the exorcist power over them.

174 biblicalstudiescenter.org/interpretation/triumphal-maccabee.htm (accessed 10 May 2021)

175 Between 1 Elul and 10 Tishrei.

There is a tangle of views concerning the identity of the war messiah, with no real certainty about the origins of the belief.[177] Whether the idea is a faint memory of the second century Jewish leader, Simon bar Kokhba, *the 'son of the star'*, who led a failed revolt against Rome or an aspirational hope that predates Christianity is still a debate.

But I personally think John uses the 'Son of Joseph' tag to deliberately inform his readers that Jesus is the war messiah. The logical answer, at least to me, is that 'Son of Joseph' and 'Son of Ephraim' are looking back to Joshua, son of Nun, the battle leader who was descended from Joseph through Ephraim. Joshua was the assistant to Moses. He loved spending time in the presence of God, often staying in the Tent of Meeting after Moses had left.[178] The first time Joshua is mentioned in Scripture is when Moses tells him to choose some men and defend the camp of Israel against the attack of the Amalekites. This was the day when

---

176 There's a strong possibility He may have fulfilled the tradition that the Messiah would be born at Migdal Eder, *the tower of the flock*, in Bethlehem. This watchtower was used by the shepherds in the service of the Temple at Jerusalem. They took care of the newborn lambs to ensure that, by swaddling them and keeping them protected in mangers, they would be unblemished and perfect for sacrificial offerings.

Another tradition may be deduced from the Book of Enoch. In it, Enoch arrives at 'the waters of Dan' (probably Banias Springs near Caesarea Philippi) and is asked to go to God on behalf of a group of fallen angels. He ascends a mountain and comes back with an answer, which basically is, 'No, you can't return to heaven.' There are overtones of Jesus doing something very similar: He leaves Caesarea Philippi to ascend a mountain where He was transfigured. Like Enoch, He is the righteous man who ascends to the court of Heaven to receive a message. This suggests that Jesus was fulfilling a traditional prophecy (doubly so, since Elijah and Moses appear with Him) as well as the Scriptural prophecy of Psalm 82.

177 See en.wikipedia.org/wiki/Messiah_ben_Joseph

178 Exodus 33:11

God was revealed as *'The Lord is my banner.'*[179] That day a scroll of remembrance was written, and it was directed that Joshua be informed of its contents. He learned the lesson of reliance on God and so, as soon as he saw the Angel outside Jericho, he didn't hesitate to obey. He took off his shoes. He was to inherit the land by putting the sole of his foot on it.

Jesus was a conqueror, like Joshua. But his way of conquest was different. Yes, His death on the cross brought redemption but we can become so focused on that, we miss what He did during His life. As the war messiah, He was continually in battle to provide an inheritance of land for the children of God. But His way of doing this was through healing the history of the land. He went to Sychar, the place where Rehoboam, grandson of David, was responsible for the kingdom being ripped apart. And there Jesus, in being proclaimed the Messiah by the Samaritans, reunited that divided kingdom. He went to Jericho which had been rebuilt at the cost of a son for the foundation and one for the gates. And there He healed two men—one of them named Bartimaeus, *son of the foundation*, and another named Zacchaeus, a tax-collector who sat at the gates. He spent two months in Gilead, at Bethany-beyond-the-Jordan, in the last winter of His life[180] and, when He left there, He retraced the journey taken by the bones of Saul and Jonathan when David had them re-interred. In doing so, He removed the ancient covenant with Sheol invoked by Saul on the

---

179 In another example of keeping 'tradition', Jesus ascended to heaven on the anniversary of this day. (The Ascension occurred ten days before Pentecost and, since Pentecost is the anniversary of the giving of the Ten Commandments at Sinai, it's simply a matter of checking what happened during the Exodus in that time-frame.) The descriptive words associated with *banner* and the scene above the battle with the Amalekites are also found in the account of the Ascension in the book of Acts.

180 Jesus went into hiding just after Hanukkah, and came out of hiding three days after receiving the news about Lazarus. This seems to be a period of forty or fifty days, with the timing being from around Christmas to February.

night before he died—and Jesus proved it was removed by raising Lazarus from the dead.

This is the task of the war messiah in John's narrative: to heal hearts and history.

PART

'Can anything good come from Nazareth?' Nathanael asked.

'Come and see,' said Philip.

When Jesus saw Nathanael approaching, He said of him,
'Here is a true Israelite, in whom there is no deceit.'

'How do You know me?' Nathanael asked.

Jesus replied, 'Before Philip called you, I saw you under the fig tree.'

'Rabbi,' Nathanael answered, 'You are the Son of God!
You are the King of Israel!'

Jesus said to him, 'Do you believe just because I told you
I saw you under the fig tree? You will see greater things than these.'
Then He declared, 'Truly, truly, I tell you,
you will all see heaven open and the angels of God
ascending and descending on the Son of Man.'

John 1:46–51 BSB

TWELVE

'Do not cling to Me,' Jesus said, 'for I have not yet ascended to the Father.
But go and tell My brothers,
"I am ascending to My Father and your Father, to My God and your God."'

Mary Magdalene went and announced to the disciples,
'I have seen the Lord!' And she told them what He had said to her.

It was the first day of the week, and that very evening,
while the disciples were together with the doors locked for fear of the Jews,
Jesus came and stood among them. 'Peace be with you!' He said to them.
After He had said this, He showed them His hands and His side.

The disciples rejoiced when they saw the Lord. Again Jesus said to them,
'Peace be with you. As the Father has sent Me, so also I am sending you.'
When He had said this, He breathed on them and said,
'Receive the Holy Spirit. If you forgive anyone his sins, they are forgiven;
if you withhold forgiveness from anyone, it is withheld.'

Now Thomas called Didymus, one of the Twelve, was not with the disciples
when Jesus came. So the other disciples told him, 'We have seen the Lord!'

But he replied, 'Unless I see the nail marks in His hands,
and put my finger where the nails have been,
and put my hand into His side, I will never believe.'

Eight days later, His disciples were once again inside with the doors locked,
and Thomas was with them. Jesus came and stood among them and said,
'Peace be with you.'

Then Jesus said to Thomas, 'Put your finger here and look at My hands.
Reach out your hand and put it into My side. Stop doubting and believe.'

Thomas replied, 'My Lord and my God!'

Jesus said to him, 'Because you have seen Me, you have believed;
blessed are those who have not seen and yet have believed.'

John 20:17-31^{BSB}

12.1 Doubts

THOMAS IS SO FAMOUS FOR HIS SUSPICION that his fellow-disciples were stuck in the denial stage of grief he's often called 'doubting Thomas'.

John has made a beautiful match here, pairing Thomas up with Nathanael. Both of them are doubters, surprised into testifying to the Lordship of Jesus:

'My Lord and my God!' Thomas exclaimed.

'You are the Son of God! You are the King of Israel!' Nathanael declared.

Jesus had just called Nathanael *'a true Israelite'*—the only time anyone is ever described that way in the gospels. 'Israel' is the name the patriarch Jacob, *deceiver*, acquired after wrestling with an angel. In just one sentence, Jesus twice alluded to Jacob as He addressed Nathanael. Both 'Israelite' and 'no deceit' are humorous wordplays saying, in effect, 'You're Israel without Jacob.' Jesus extended the allusion when He mentioned angels ascending and descending—just as Jacob had seen in his dream at Bethel.

That is a crucial hint about the spiritual pairing in these two scenes. It's all about Israel and the tribes descended from him. But the theme is doubt. So John is prompting his readers to recall a time when the tribes of Israel were subject to doubt. The obvious stand-out example is the incident when the tribes, camped on the border of the Promised Land, sent out twelve spies on a forty-day reconnaissance mission. On their return, ten of the twelve spies expressed extreme doubt about the ability of the Israelites to take up the inheritance God had promised them:

> 'The land that we've explored is one that devours its inhabitants. All the people whom we observed were giants. We also saw the Nephilim, the descendants of Anak. Compared to the Nephilim, as we see things, we're like grasshoppers, and that's their opinion of us!'
>
> Numbers 13:32–33[ISV]

Only Joshua and Caleb dissented from this false report, averring their belief that the Israelites were able to take the country. Ten against two: ten who doubted, two who had faith.

As we look at the story of Thomas, we see these numbers reversed. Ten of Jesus' twelve disciples were holding firm, while two had doubts. Judas had such overwhelming doubts that he had taken his own life.

Yet this is another healing of a rupture in history—a theme consistently proclaimed throughout John's gospel. The greatest social and spiritual breach of all time occurred in the Garden of Eden, but Jesus reversed that moment in the garden outside His tomb. Instead of God the Gardener coming to look for mankind, a representative of mankind came looking for God and mistook Him for a gardener.

The second greatest social and spiritual fissure in history was healed when Jesus walked the road to Emmaus.[181] And the third

---

[181] This is the complete destruction of the tribal brotherhood and the first beginnings of a rival priesthood as a result of the actions of Jonathan, the grandson of Moses. Jesus reverses this terrible breach by walking the same road at the same time of day but, as always, changing the story's ending.

was set-up when He appeared to His disciples in the Upper Room while Thomas was absent. He was intent on healing the defilement of the land brought about the ten spies whose doubts led to thirty-eight extra years of wandering in the wilderness for the people of Israel. Only when Thomas acknowledged the King did the wounds of the past find a deep resolution in the present. This story is not just about Thomas, it's about all of Israel. It's about Jesus, the Author and Finisher of our faith. He is, as we have seen, not just the One who completed the unfinished tasks of Elijah and John the Baptiser, Moses and Joshua, David and Saul—and ours too, incidentally, when we fall short—He is also the One who rewrites the stories. He is the Poet who shapes the verse and changes the endings into happily-ever-after healings. He sits on the throne, saying:

> 'Behold, I make all things new.'
>
> Revelation 21:5[BSB]

12.2 Introductions, Inheritance and Identity

'Rabbi,' Nathanael answered. 'You are the Son of God! You are the King of Israel!'

John 1:49^{BSB}

'My Lord and my God!' Thomas exclaimed.

John 20:28^{NLT}

THE FIRST TIME ANY DISCIPLE addresses Jesus as God—God incarnate, God in the flesh—it is Thomas. Nathanael limited himself to *'Son of God'* after Andrew had confided his belief that he'd found the Messiah.

All throughout his first chapter, John presents us with a season of introductions and identification. The Baptiser was quizzed about his identity and then, identifying the Lamb of God, he introduced his disciples to Jesus. The following day, Andrew went to find Simon to introduce him in turn to Jesus. On the day after that, Philip looked for Nathanael to likewise introduce him to Jesus.

As soon as Jesus met Simon, He told him a new thing concerning his identity: he'd be known as Cephas. Similarly Nathanael received a revelation about his identity. Nathanael is usually translated *gift of God*. Matthew, Mark and Luke—in both his gospel and the account in Acts—have Bartholomew where John has Nathanael. It would make much more sense to have Bartholomew named here in the pair with Thomas, because Bartholomew means *son of Tolmai*. Tolmai, or Talmai, is one possible root of the name Thomas. Talmai is a perfect fit here because it's a name appearing in the story of the ten doubting spies. One of the giants who caused extreme misgivings for the spies was named Talmai.[182] In the historical reversal Jesus had engaged with, the name associated with *projecting doubt* now became linked with *harbouring doubt*.

But John chose to forgo this nifty word-match of Thomas and Bartholomew. Personally I'm inclined to believe he chose Nathanael with great forethought because he wanted to evoke its other possible meaning: *God fixes*.

He wanted to say that Jesus came to mend the world. To bind up the broken-hearted, yes, but also to heal the broken bones of history itself. To ring in the wondrous inheritance of the children of God and the sons of Israel.

> *The whole creation is on tiptoe to see the wonderful sight of the sons of God coming into their own. The world of creation cannot as yet see reality, not because it chooses to be blind, but because in God's purpose it has been so limited—yet it has been given hope. And the hope is that in the end the whole of created life will be rescued from the tyranny of change and decay, and have its share in that magnificent liberty which can only belong to the children of God!*
>
> Romans 8:19–21[PHPS]

The odd thing about Nathanael is that Jesus, on meeting him, spoke of a destiny entirely wrapped around the name Jacob.

---

182 It's also the name of Absalom's grandfather and David's father-in-law, the king of Geshur. Perhaps this is a hint there was nephilim ancestry in Absalom's bloodline. Certainly we are given the impression there was something odd about him genetically—to do with the amount of hair he grew each year and which, in the end, contributed to his death.

Israel… no deceit… angels ascending and descending… these are all evocative of the patriarch Jacob.

More subtly, in the background, there are still more echoes of Jacob, *deceiver, supplanter, swindler* from *one who grasps the heel*. He was given it because he came out of womb holding onto the heel of his twin brother, Esau.

Now recall that the word for *heel* is also *if*, that iconic symbol from Delphi that signified *choice*. So the sense of *he who grasps the heel* is not simply a foot-grabber but the *one who opportunistically snatches at gain through other people's choices*. That describes Jacob quite well, with the additional proviso that he was always on the lookout for the right moment to apply pressure when it came to other people's choices. He was an expert manipulator—though he met his match in his uncle Laban.

Jacob's name is associated with the heel—or the foot. And throughout the first and last chapters of John's gospel the foot symbolises inheritance. Indeed, that's a prime aspect of Jesus' words to Nathanael: 'I saw you under the fig tree.'

To *'sit under your own vine and your own fig tree'* was a proverbial expression[183] for peace and prosperity, enjoying the fruit of your labour and the produce of your own land. It was about contentment and a celebration of the deep and tranquil shalom that came with the blessings of your own inheritance.

Here the thread of inheritance—symbolised by the imprint of a foot on the land, by a loosened sandal, and by the net of 153 fish—re-emerges in the image of the fig tree.

The archaeologist Adam Zertal thought that the enormous sandal-shaped sanctuaries built in the Jordan Valley and on Mount Ebal, above Shechem, represented the footprints of Yahweh in the

---

[183] See 1 Kings 4:25; Micah 4:4; Zechariah 3:10.

land.[184] Perhaps too they were the embodiment of the promise made to Abram and Joshua that you will be given the place where your feet walk. Zertal also considers that the word 'chug' or 'hug' for *festival* across various Semitic languages ultimately derives its meaning from *encircle*. These 'footprints' in the land were bordered by stone-walled walkways for people to walk around the outline, singing while sacrifices were offered at the tabernacle in the centre.

There are three special pilgrimages in Judaism called 'regelim'— Passover, Pentecost and Tabernacles. 'Regelim' means *holiday* but it comes from the word for *foot*.[185] Zertal believed the words for *pilgrimage* derived from the foot-shaped structures in the landscape. He pointed out that, in the ancient world, the foot also held significance as a symbol of ownership of territory, control over an enemy, connection between people and land, and presence of the Deity.

For the people of Israel, there was a special festival that evoked the time of rest and peace associated with *sitting under your own vine or your own fig tree*. It was Sukkot, one of the three 'regelim', also known as the Feast of Booths or the Festival of Tabernacles. And, no surprise for the time structure of John's narrative, it was just three days away.

And it wasn't coincidence that Jesus was about to set out for Galilee to attend a wedding at Cana.

Of course, neither is it coincidence that, in backing up from the end of John's gospel, another of the three 'regelim' is about to be prominent: the festival of the Passover. But more significant still are the events of the feast of First Fruits.

---

[184] www.thetorah.com/article/gilgal-yhwhs-footprints-in-the-land-of-israel (accessed 28 November 2021)

[185] www.israel21c.org/ancient-foot-provides-insight-to-israelite-pilgrimages/ (accessed 28 December 2021)

12.3 Ascending

The chapter divisions of the Bible are not part of the original text; they are paratext that was only added in the thirteenth century. In the middle of the sixteenth century, editors started to sub-divide the chapters into verses. Within the Hebrew Scriptures, these components of paratext often differ between Jewish and Christian traditions.

So it wasn't until well after a millennium had passed before John's gospel was segmented into chapters—which is why the pairing of the first chapter doesn't link neatly to the last chapter but flows backwards into the second last chapter. The comment of Jesus to Nathanael about seeing angels ascending and descending on the Son of Man has its natural twin in His direction to the Magdalene: *'Do not cling to Me for I have not yet ascended to the Father. But go and tell My brothers, "I am ascending to My Father and your Father, to My God and your God."'*

This happens in the garden outside the tomb. What happens there is the encapsulation of so much history and prophecy in such a short space that it must be left to another book. However, let's look at just a small snippet that impacts on the earlier scene with Nathanael.

The garden outside the tomb is a reversal of the story in Eden where the divine Gardener came looking for humanity, who had in their shame just sewn leaves from a fig tree together to form clothing. Nathanael's fig tree, in paralleling the trees of the garden outside the tomb, is therefore more than a symbol of a state of rest and prosperity for the nation, it is an image of the return to Eden. It's a picture of mankind climbing up to and passing through the gateway guarded by the flaming swords of the cherubim, then wandering through His well-watered garden until we find Him and realise we have come into His presence on His holy mountain.

'I have not yet ascended to the Father,' Jesus said to the Magdalene. In other words: 'I haven't climbed the ladder, I haven't gone up the ramp through the veil, I haven't yet disarmed the cherubim and opened the gate back into the Garden of which this present earthly one is a sign and a symbol, and I promised Nathanael I'd fix this, so please let him and the others know what's going on. I'll be back soon.'

Of all the enigmatic sayings in the gospels, the words of Jesus at this time are some of the most mysterious. Why did He tell Mary not to touch Him when, eight days later, He would encourage Thomas to do so? The timing, according to Eli Lizorkin-Eyzenberg, is very significant. It's because it takes seven days to ordain a priest and, during that time, it is vital to maintain complete ceremonial cleanness in order not to be disqualified.[186]

This then is the moment when John presents us with the priestly messiah. His gospel openly calls Jesus the war messiah, the Son of Joseph, as well as the Son of God, Son of Man, the Word, the Light, and the Life. In subtle ways, he also presents Him as the royal messiah, the Son of David, but without using that

---

186 See: weekly.israelbiblecenter.com/mary-couldnt-touch-jesus/ (accessed 27 December 2021)

terminology. Here he proclaims Him as the High Priest of the line of Melchizedek.

Jesus, by His own admission, was preparing to ascend the ramp into the Holy of Holies in heavenly places. The unique word, 'sullam', translated *ladder* in the vision of Jacob at Bethel is probably better rendered *ramp* because steps were forbidden within the sanctuary on the off-chance the priest's genitalia were exposed as his garment lifted.[187]

Jesus took His own blood into the holy place in the heavenly sanctuary as the offering. The death-wielding cherubim who guarded the mercy seat, as well as the gate into Eden, would recognise the authority of His blood—that of the scapegoat—and let Him pass. He was seeking divine validation of His appointment as the High Priest according to the order of Melchizedek. Had Mary touched Him at this point, there was a risk the offering would be defiled and the consecration made profane. But, over a week later, once the time of ritual purification was complete, it would no longer be an issue to invite Thomas to touch Him.

The appointment of Jesus as the High Priest has a significant bearing on His actions as soon as He returned from heaven. In the forty days after His resurrection, we know only of seven events in His life during that time. The record is sparse and, although John admits that many other things happened he didn't write about, I for one am left wondering what Jesus was doing during that time—beyond the works we know about.

We know He appeared to five hundred people at one time, but we know nothing about the circumstances. We don't know where or when it happened.

---

187 It's because of this command that I believe David was wrong to defend his actions in dancing 'naked' before the Ark to Michal. She was wrong to hold him in contempt, but he was wrong to justify himself.

We know He appeared to Mary Magdalene in the garden, to Peter at some unknown point the same day, to the disciples in the Upper Room on two occasions eight days apart, and to seven of the disciples for breakfast on the shore of the Sea of Galilee. And of course, there was that strange and beautiful encounter on the road to Emmaus.

12.4 The Emmaus Mending

John doesn't tell the story of the walk to Emmaus. But I believe Luke's account only makes sense in the light of Jesus' recent appointment as High Priest, so let's look at it anyway.

> *That same day two of Jesus' disciples were going to the village of Emmaus, which was about eleven kilometres from Jerusalem. As they were talking and thinking about what had happened, Jesus came near and started walking along beside them. But they did not know who He was.*
>
> *Jesus asked them, 'What were you talking about as you walked along?'*
>
> *The two of them stood there looking sad and gloomy. Then the one named Cleopas asked Jesus, 'Are you the only person from Jerusalem who didn't know what was happening there these last few days?'*
>
> *'What do you mean?' Jesus asked.*
>
> *They answered: 'Those things that happened to Jesus from Nazareth. By what He did and said He showed that He was a powerful prophet, who pleased God and all the people. Then the chief priests and our leaders had Him arrested and sentenced to die on a cross. We had hoped that He would be the one to set Israel free! But it has already been three days*

since all this happened. Some women in our group surprised us. They had gone to the tomb early in the morning, but did not find the body of Jesus. They came back, saying they had seen a vision of angels who told them that He is alive. Some men from our group went to the tomb and found it just as the women had said. But they didn't see Jesus either.'

Then Jesus asked the two disciples, 'Why can't you understand? How can you be so slow to believe all that the prophets said? Didn't you know that the Messiah would have to suffer before He was given His glory?' Jesus then explained everything written about Himself in the Scriptures, beginning with the Law of Moses and the Books of the Prophets.

When the two of them came near the village where they were going, Jesus seemed to be going farther. They begged Him, 'Stay with us! It's already late, and the sun is going down.' So Jesus went into the house to stay with them.

'After Jesus sat down to eat, He took some bread. He blessed it and broke it. Then He gave it to them. At once they knew who He was, but He disappeared. They said to each other, 'When He talked with us along the road and explained the Scriptures to us, didn't it warm our hearts?' So they got up and returned to Jerusalem.

The two disciples found the eleven apostles and the others gathered together. And they learned from the group that the Lord was really alive and had appeared to Peter. Then the disciples from Emmaus told what happened on the road and how they knew He was the Lord when He broke the bread.

Luke 24:13–35^{CEV}

The Emmaus story puzzled me for a very long time. It just didn't sit 'right', psychologically speaking. I mean, if you had been tortured, died an excruciating death, been gone for three days before being raised from the dead, would your first action be to head off for a hike out of town and meet two random disciples? Wouldn't you make it a priority to comfort your grieving mother and friends?

And if your mother and friends aren't your top priority, just what exactly is going on during that walk that shunts everything else aside? Who are these disciples—or rather, who do they represent? And why did Jesus make this the very first item on His to-do list once He got back from heaven?

I suspect that it was vitally important that Jesus be a priest for the trip to Emmaus—and so the mending He was intent on bringing about couldn't be accomplished until this time. Like all the other ruptures in history that He repaired, the fine detail is important.

- It's late afternoon, getting on towards sundown.

- Two people are heading out from Jerusalem through the countryside about seven miles, when they are joined by a third.

- One disciple is named Cleopas and he's probably the same person as Clopas, whose wife was present at the crucifixion. Early Christian tradition maintained that the unnamed other disciple who accompanied Cleopas to Emmaus was indeed his wife, Mary.

- In addition, it identifies Cleopas as the uncle of Jesus and brother of Joseph. This relationship is important because it means the 'hometown' of Cleopas was Bethlehem—just as it had been for Joseph.

Is there any story in Scripture that starts with a man and his wife heading about seven miles past Jerusalem in the late afternoon—any tragedy that needs a new happily-ever-after ending of joy and redemption? Of course there is. That story was recognised from the earliest Christian times and, in the versions used by believers of the Septuagint—the Greek translations of Hebrew Scriptures—the wording of Judges 19:14–15 was tweaked just a little to match Luke's description of the scene.[188]

The fact that Jesus prioritised this walk above all other matters suggests that, the tragedy of Eden aside, He was working to repair the greatest calamity in all history. The Fall was the greatest disaster ever for humanity, but what is the next? We might suspect the first murder, the first rape, the first war. And, yes, murder, rape and war are all involved but none of them were the 'first'.

The reason Jesus needed to be a High Priest to bind up this wound was because it was a Levite from Bethlehem who caused it. That priest opened up a rift in the tribal brotherhood so enormous it went on, violence breeding violence, for generations.

Moses had welded together all the clans of Israel into a league of tribes during the forty years in the wilderness. But all his work was destroyed in a moment by his grandson, Jonathan.

With his concubine and servant in tow, Jonathan had left his father-in-law's home in Bethlehem on his way to the hill country of Ephraim. Passing Jerusalem in the late afternoon, he reached the town of Gibeah just as the sun was setting. There was no hospitable welcome waiting—although they did eventually find lodging for the night, the house was soon surrounded by

---

[188] See: Carsten Thiede, *The Emmaus Mystery—Discovering Evidence for the Risen Christ*, Continuum Books, 2005. Thiede points out that the *Codex Alexandrinus* altered the Greek text of Judges 19:9 so that it reads just like Luke 24:29. He also comments that modern translators have seen the parallel too and given the verses identical wording. I believe Thiede must have been referring to German translators in this instance because this parallelism is not reflected in any English versions I have consulted.

townspeople wanting the Levite to come out so they could have sex with him. Instead he sent out his concubine to appease them. She died early in the morning, following a night of gang rape. Her final act was to reach out to touch the threshold of the lodging—the sacred cornerstone that was not to be touched. In doing so, she accused her husband and the host of the lodging of breaking covenant with her. Under the rites of hospitality at the time, and the covenant associated with it, they should both have defended her to the death—but instead they made her the sacrifice to save themselves.

Jonathan sent out a gruesome call for war. As a result, eleven tribes mustered to fight the men of Gibeah. The tribe of Benjamin chose to come to protect the town. At the end of the conflict, there were so few survivors of Benjamin that they numbered just 1 out of 100 compared to their pre-war tally. 99% of the tribe had been exterminated. The rebuilding involved more violence, more warfare, more pain.

So, perhaps wisely, Jonathan left the hill country of Ephraim. He went north, stealing a silver ephod—a copy of the high priest's breastplate—from his employer and accepting the position of a priest for the entire tribe of Dan. He and his descendants established a rival priesthood, involving idolatrous worship with a golden calf at this northern shrine. And for centuries, a vicious feud existed between the people of Gibeah and the people of Bethlehem. Each blamed the other for the genocidal war. The mistrust persisted for generations. The dark jealousy of Saul of Gibeah towards David of Bethlehem is entwined with this mutual hatred.

This is the backstory that Jesus the High Priest was intent on mending. It seems almost ridiculously simple that this healing of history hinges on a mere offer of genuine hospitality. It could so easily have turned out differently. Even though all Jesus had to do was walk the same road at the same time of day with a man and his wife who hailed from Bethlehem, they still needed to ask Him to come in and dine with them in order to change the storyline. Because the covenant wouldn't be ratified until they broke bread together.

And perhaps because the wife of Cleopas had faithfully and steadfastly stood by Jesus at the Cross, there was never any question they would be false to that covenant.

The journey to Emmaus is not just delightful comedy and heart-warming consolation in the midst of grief, it is the first atoning action of Jesus as the High Priest of the Jewish nation.

12.5 Full Circle

John finishes his gospel with a scene set in Galilee, a district meaning *circuit, ring* or *cylinder*. Appropriately for a literary text with a concentric construction, it ends on a roll. That's because, like Gilgal, the name Galilee comes from the Hebrew root, 'galal', *to roll.*

Although the setting doesn't bring us back perfectly to the beginning in Gilead at Bethany-beyond-the-Jordan, it does return us to the person of Elijah. Just as John the Baptiser, even while he right in the place anciently known as the Brook Cherith, denies being the Elijah-who-is-to-come, so too does John the Apostle. He is insistent that, just because Jesus said, *'If I want him to remain until I come, what is that to you?'* that doesn't mean he will be like Elijah and not see death.

Of course, the final line about all the books that would need to be written to catalogue all the doings—*the poetry*—of Jesus links back to the opening description of 'The Word'. John's circle is complete—like a joyful choir of revellers treading around and around the outline of a giant footstep in the landscape, his gospel goes around and around like a song of praise.

Through the partnering of the names, the numbers, the themes and the incidents in the first and last (and a bit of the second last) chapters, John identifies Jesus of Nazareth as the Word, the Light, the Life, Immanuel, the Christ, the new Moses, the new Jacob, the new Israel, the new Joshua, the Son of Man, the Son of God, the war messiah known as the 'Son of Joseph', the priestly messiah who is like Melchizedek, and also the Elijah-who-is-to-come.

And this is just his beginning salvo. Beauty, truth and joy unfold with further spectacular radiance as the witness of his 'ring' continues.

This series continues in Volume 2:

ISBN 978-1-925380-67-5

Mary and Mary—the mother and the Magdalene—feature in the second and second-last chapters of John's gospel. In the episodes involving them, quotes from one of Scripture's most famous sagas appear: the story of Joseph of the coat-of-many-colours. This parallelism shows Jesus as the true bearer of Joseph's title, the 'Saviour of the World'. Jesus fulfills many prophecies in His interaction with the women and proves Himself not just the redeemer of Time, but its Lord.

Volume 3 coming late 2024:

ISBN 978-1-925380-76-7

THE LUSTRAL WATERS continues to explore the symmetrical chiastic patterning in the fourth gospel. One of John's hidden themes is the passing of an ancient prophetic or governmental mantle from the keeping of Jesus on to various members of the family of faith.

In this third chapter, John brings up the legacy of Moses. He relies on his reader's knowledge of the extraordinary fame of Buni ben Gurion, nicknamed Nicodemus, the 'Man of the Breakthrough', to augment his previous revelation about the summoning of time and also to unveil a critical understanding of what it means to be born from above.

Other Books by Anne Hamilton

STRATEGIES FOR THE THRESHOLD series

Dealing with Python: Spirit of Constriction (with Arpana Dev Sangamithra)
Dealing with Ziz: Spirit of Forgetting
Name Covenant: Invitation to Friendship
Hidden in the Cleft: True and False Refuge
Dealing with Leviathan: Spirit of Retaliation
Dealing with Resheph: Spirit of Trouble (with Irenie Senior)
Dealing with Azazel: Spirit of Rejection
Dealing with Belial: Spirit of Abuse and Armies (with Janice Speirs)
Dealing with Kronos: Spirit of Time and Abuse (with Janice Speirs)
Dealing with Lilith: Spirit of Dispossession

DEVOTIONAL THEOLOGY series

God's Poetry: The Identity & Destiny Encoded in Your Name
God's Panoply: The Armour of God & the Kiss of Heaven
God's Pageantry: The Threshold Guardians & the Covenant Defender
God's Pottery: The Sea of Names & the Pierced Inheritance
God's Priority: World-Mending & Generational Testing
More Precious than Pearls (with Natalie Tensen)
As Resplendent as Rubies (with Natalie Tensen)
As Exceptional as Sapphires (with Donna Ho)
Spiritual Legal Rights (with Janice Sergison)
Core Values: Love (with Rebekah Robinson)
Core Values: Joy (with Rebekah Robinson)
Core Values: Peace (with Rebekah Robinson)

JESUS AND THE HEALING OF HISTORY series

Like Wildflowers, Suddenly
Bent World, Bright Wings
Silk Shadows, Rings of Gold
Where His Feet Pass
The Singing Silence
In the Meshes of the Net
Interpreted by Love

Grace Drops with Anne podcast: https://gracedropswithanne.com

www.ingramcontent.com/pod-product-compliance
Lightning Source LLC
Chambersburg PA
CBHW070641120526
44590CB00013BA/815